What is "the system" and how should we change it?

Transform the System:
A Work in Progress

Wade Lee Hudson

www.TransformTheSystem.org

Transform the System: A Work in Progress

Wade Lee Hudson — 1st Ed.

Published in the United States of America

ISBN-13: 978-1986126106

CONTENTS:

Preface

What is "the system" and how should we change it? This draft declaration offers an answer. It aims to clarify a root cause of needless suffering — our social system — and proposes methods that individuals and communities can use to transform our society.

This work-in-progress is presented as food-for-thought, not the final word. Others could compose a better response. Hopefully, someone will.

In the meantime, you're invited to help improve this work or suggest your own proposals for action. You can comment on this work online, submit your own essay, or participate in a workshop to evaluate it and agree on feedback. For more information about those options, see TransformTheSystem.org.

Ideally this effort will prompt one or more strong organizing committees to initiate some of the projects recommended here. After publishing this booklet independently, we may seek a publisher with a larger distribution network for the next version, which could include essays written by others addressing the same issues.

With this draft declaration, at the age of 73, I sum up conclusions from my life experience. In school, my main areas of study were political science, psychology, and theology. Those three subjects have been my main interests ever since.

After receiving my bachelor's degree, a field major in social sciences, and studying in seminary for two years, I was employed by various non-profit organizations for twenty years. Then I discovered that I could manage financially working part-time as a cab driver, until I retired last year. That work left me free to do whatever community work I wanted to do.

Throughout my life, the consistent thread has been the effort to nurture communities whose members share basic beliefs, help one another become better human beings, and engage in political action to improve public policies. My efforts have taken many forms. Some have been more successful than others. All have been learning experiences. My community organizing history is summarized at the end of this draft declaration in the "About the Author" section.

I look back most warmly on a neighborhood organizing project that was rooted in a volunteer-based food cooperative. We recruited shoppers to participate in square dances, clam bakes on the beach, volleyball games in the park, door-to-door voter registration, and get-out-the-vote. It was a lively, rich sense of community.

One failure was an effort to stop state legislation that was designed to force cities to increase public-transit fares, which hurt low-income passengers. When we met with our representative, he wouldn't even discuss the issue and we got nowhere.

Some twenty friends and associates have contributed to this effort so far. I hope you join us.

Introduction

America faces many problems. Addressing the root cause of those challenges requires us to improve ourselves, our culture, and our society. The more we improve as individuals, the more we improve the world — in every sphere. The more the world improves, the more we improve. Those efforts reinforce each other.

Human beings are conflicted. We're inclined to trust, which leads to love and cooperation, and we're prone to fear, which leads to anger and domination. Both trust and fear are essential. A balance between the two is needed. When we're thrown off, restoring balance requires self-awareness.

William James argued that no philosophy of life is adequate if it refuses to account for "the evil facts" that are "a genuine portion of reality," which "may after all be the best key to life's significance, and possibly the only openers of our eyes to the deepest levels of truth."[1] To deal with reality we have to see it for what it is, even when it's painful.

James Baldwin said:

> *A day will come when you will trust you more than you do now and you will trust me more than you do now. And we can trust each other…. I really do believe that we can all become better than we are. I know we can. But the price is enormous and people are not yet willing to pay.*[2]

One price we must pay is to acknowledge our weaknesses, admit our mistakes and resolve to avoid repeating them, and accept failure when our efforts fall short. That requires self-understanding.

Trust, compassion, and cooperation are growing in certain parts of America. But fear, anger, and efforts to dominate are on the rise too. By inflaming fear, politicians get re-elected, the media sells advertising, and as people get distracted financial interests gain more freedom to do whatever they want. Americans are getting sucked into a self-perpetuating downward spiral of fear, anger, division, top-down domination, and more fear. Countering that threat and nurturing trust will require mutual support that nurtures self-awareness and self-development.

Our personal problems are human problems. No one suffers from all of them, but if we're honest, most of us will acknowledge that we're troubled by at least some of them. If you face those that apply to you, you can work on them. We all need to become better human beings.

Far too often, in our inner world, we:

- focus on the outer world and neglect the non-material, or spiritual;
- avoid critical self-examination and don't work enough on our self-development;
- minimize our own responsibility and scapegoat others;
- are judgmental toward others and ourselves;
- let our anger get the best of us;
- assume we're essentially superior human beings;
- label others, place them in boxes, and keep them there;
- identify primarily with our tribe and forget our common humanity;
- react to others based on their skin color, gender, or some other arbitrary physical characteristic;
- dwell in the realm of ideas and neglect feelings;
- discriminate against people who have less education or income;
- envy and resent those who have more education or income;
- stereotype people who live in a different region of the country;
- don't try to better understand those who disagree with us;

- are unable to agree to disagree and still communicate fruitfully;
- assume some one person must always be in charge;
- are too concerned about our self-interest and our family's;
- are convinced we have the final answer;
- are unable to see many sides to the same issue.

In our social interactions, far too often we:
- talk too much and don't listen enough;
- fail to engage in soulful, heart-to-heart, mutual dialog;
- spend too much time gossiping, telling stories about our past, or lecturing;
- don't take enough time to develop good friendships;
- reduce others to tools to be used;
- don't support others in their personal growth efforts;
- engage in logical arguments and ignore underlying universal irrationality;
- are mean, nasty, or rude;
- inflame fear and anger;
- spend most of our time dominating or submitting;
- Indulge in dog-eat-dog competition;
- seek more power over others;
- only take care of ourselves and our family and neglect others.

And in our political activism, we:
- aim to crush opponents;
- give up on finding common ground, compromise, and reconciliation;
- forget to take care of ourselves and burn out;
- believe winning is everything;
- concentrate too hard on having an impact;
- don't pay enough attention to *how* we work;
- Overlook that means need to be consistent with ends;
- fail to consider if short-term goals are consistent with long-term goals;
- make the better the enemy of the good;

- work with organizations that won't form coalitions;
- don't nurture supportive communities that stay together and attract others;
- are too willing to impose suffering on innocent bystanders;
- assume that leaders are those who mobilize followers;
- indulge in either/or thinking, rather than both/and;
- fail to seek win/win solutions.

Those attitudes are learned. They're largely the result of social conditioning. We need not beat ourselves up or blame ourselves for our weaknesses. We're all victims. With intentional effort, however, conditioning can be unlearned. We can learn to control our divisive instincts and build up our cooperative instincts.

Chances for success will be increased if we understand the social system that we're up against. Elizabeth Warren brought the crowd to its feet at the 2012 Democratic Convention when she declared, "The system is rigged."[3] Donald Trump used the phrase to win the White House.[4] Bernie Sanders almost gained the Democratic nomination with his criticisms of "the system."[5] Yet there's little agreement on a key question: What is "the system" and how should we change it?

This draft declaration offers an answer to that question. It argues:

1. Our institutions, our culture, and we ourselves as individuals are woven together into a self-perpetuating social system: the System.

2. The primary purpose of the System is to enable individuals to gain more status, wealth, and power over others by climbing social ladders.

3. America needs to transform itself into a compassionate community dedicated to the welfare of all humanity, our own people, the environment, and life itself.

4. Then Americans can create new institutions and reform existing institutions, our culture, and ourselves to serve that purpose.

5. That effort will require new ways of organizing political action.

6. Activists need to **set aside time** to support one another in their self-development.

That approach is all-inclusive. It pursues the interests of every unit: individual, family, community, workplace, city, state, nation, mankind, the environment, and all life. It asks no unit to sacrifice its true interests. If we all benefit, we all benefit. It does not try to impose a blueprint. It commits to experiment with ways forward until we find a path to achieve that universal goal. With a balance between trust and fear, everyone involved can have a voice.

+++++

This draft declaration is rooted in the values expressed in the Charter for Compassion,[6] the Universal Declaration of Human Rights,[7] and the philosophy of Dr. Martin Luther King, Jr.[8] The Charter, which has been signed by more than two million people throughout the world, affirms:

The principle of compassion lies at the heart of all religious, ethical and spiritual traditions, calling us always to treat all others as we wish to be treated ourselves. Compassion impels us to work tirelessly to alleviate the suffering of our fellow creatures, to dethrone ourselves from the centre of our world and put another there, and to honour the inviolable sanctity of every single human being, treating everybody, without exception, with absolute justice, equity and respect....

We urgently need to make compassion a clear, luminous and dynamic force in our polarized world. Rooted in a principled determination to transcend selfishness, compassion can break down political, dogmatic, ideological and religious boundaries. Born of our deep interdependence, compassion is essential to human relationships and to a fulfilled humanity. It is the path to enlightenment, and indispensable to the creation of a just economy and a peaceful global community.

The Universal Declaration of Human Rights, which was adopted by the United Nations General Assembly in 1948, affirms "the inherent dignity" and "the equal and inalienable rights of all members of the human family." Article One declares, "All human beings are born free and equal in dignity and rights. They are endowed with reason and conscience and should act towards one another in a spirit of brotherhood."

According to the King Center:

> *Dr. King's Beloved Community is a global vision, in which all people can share in the wealth of the earth. In the Beloved Community, poverty, hunger and homelessness will not be tolerated because international standards of human decency will not allow it. Racism and all forms of discrimination, bigotry and prejudice will be replaced by an all-inclusive spirit of sisterhood and brotherhood. In the Beloved Community, international disputes will be resolved by peaceful conflict-resolution and reconciliation of adversaries, instead of military power. Love and trust will triumph over fear and hatred. Peace with justice will prevail over war and military conflict.*
>
> *Dr. King's Beloved Community was not devoid of interpersonal, group or international conflict. Instead he recognized that conflict was an inevitable part of human experience. But he believed that conflicts could be resolved peacefully and adversaries could be reconciled through a mutual, determined commitment to nonviolence. No conflict, he believed, need erupt in violence. And all conflicts in The Beloved Community should end with reconciliation of adversaries cooperating together in a spirit of friendship and goodwill....*

The King Philosophy is founded on the Six Principles of Nonviolence:

1. *Nonviolence is a way of life for courageous people.*
2. *Nonviolence seeks to win friendship and understanding.*
3. *Nonviolence seeks to defeat injustice not people.*
4. *Nonviolence holds that suffering can educate and transform.*
5. *Nonviolence chooses love instead of hate.*
6. *Nonviolence believes that the universe is on the side of justice.*

Dr. King's Six Steps for Nonviolent Social Change are:

1. *Information gathering.*
2. *Education.*
3. *Personal commitment.*
4. *Discussion/negotiation.*
5. *Direct action.*
6. *Reconciliation.*

The goal of Kingian nonviolence is not to defeat enemies. Rooted in compassion, we leave the door open to reconciliation. We hate the sin without hating the sinner. With firm compassion, we restrain those who violate the rights of others. With constructive criticism, we challenge selfishness. With determined effort, we improve our mental and moral qualities — our character — and restructure our society to make it more democratic. The goal is the Beloved Community.

Numerous organizations integrate personal and social transformation with efforts that require extensive training and generally involve full-time, paid staff.[9] This draft declaration aims to take some of that knowledge out into the world in a way that can quickly enrich anyone's life. The twelve-step movement, using a fairly simple tool, demonstrates the potential of that approach.[10] A simpler tool might spread even more quickly and help activists support one another in their self-development. For many people, that interaction could be a first step that leads to deeper work, both personally and politically.

In "Our Elites Still Don't Get It," David Brooks wrote:

The branches of individual rights are sprawling, but the roots of common obligation are withering away. Freedom without covenant becomes selfishness. And that's what we see at the top of society, in our politics and the financial crisis. Freedom without connection becomes alienation. And that's what we see at the bottom of society — frayed communities, broken families, opiate addiction. Freedom without a unifying national narrative becomes distrust, polarization and permanent political war.... Change has to come at the communal, emotional and moral level.[11]

If we ordinary Americans strengthen ourselves, we can improve our ability to work together and build broad, massive grassroots coalitions that act together in unison. We can address the many crises we face and enable everyone to become more fully human.

America's major problems include:
- Big Money has too much power.[12]
- Our society creates inherited inequality.[13]
- Many groups are oppressed due to their skin color or who they are.[14]
- Wages are stagnant.[15]
- Technology displaces workers.[16]
- The poor are divided by race and whites are divided by class, leaving us without enough unity to act effectively.[17]
- We're losing the battle against global warming.[18]
- Growing individualism isolates individuals and undermines community.[19]
- More people have fewer friends with whom they discuss personal problems.[20]
- Our culture is becoming more selfish.[21]

- The war on terror creates more terrorists than it kills.[22]

Those problems are interrelated and share a common root cause: our social system. Understanding that system and agreeing on how to change it are critical.

To build a broad movement that is powerful enough to have a major impact, we need to bring to the table as wide a range of opinions as possible, clarify our differences, and seek agreement on some concrete action. That effort might lead to a campaign to push for positive changes in national policy that are backed by majorities of rank-and-file Republicans, Independents, and Democrats (many such proposals do exist).[23] As he reports in *Collaborating with the Enemy: How to Work with People You Don't Agree with or Like or Trust*, Adam Kahane and his Reos Partners have had success facilitating that kind of process.[24] We need not agree on everything. We can continue to have many disagreements, and still agree on specific steps to improve our situation.

From the point of view of this draft declaration, systemic transformation would enable America to correct mistakes, more fully realize her ideals, and reinforce her best traditions. With that foundation, Americans could more easily respect authority (legitimate power), be loyal to one another, honor the sacred, defend liberty, assure that everyone gets a fair shake, protect the weak and vulnerable, punish those who are abusive, and reward those who do good. Those are American values.

To help develop a transformation strategy, this draft declaration addresses the following questions:

1. What is "the system?" Does it have a central purpose? If so, what is it? How is it structured and how does it operate?
2. How do we, as individuals and with our organizations, reinforce the system?
3. Would a transformed society have a new mission? If so, what should it be?

4. How would a transformed society be organized? What would it look like?
5. How can activists improve how we operate? How can we overcome divisions, such as those shaped by race, class, and gender? What strategies will help us succeed?
6. What forms of leadership are most effective? Is leadership always defined by the ability to mobilize others? Must leaders always be in charge? How should victims of oppression have more voice in how to deal with it?
7. What easy-to-learn method could be widely used to provide mutual support for self-development and political activism?

Preliminary answers to those questions are suggested as food for thought in the following chapters. You're invited to comment on those answers at the end of each chapter at TransformTheSystem.org. If you want to submit your own answer as an essay, feel free to post it elsewhere and include a link to it in your comment.

Whatever your political and spiritual perspective, you're welcome to participate. The aim here is to find widely shared beliefs that could be the foundation for massive, grassroots movements. You can participate either as an individual or with a group that works in person, online, or with conference calls. If possible, please discuss these issues with others and formulate a joint response. Thinking together is a great way to think. You can buy copies of this booklet on Amazon or print copies from the website.

The proposals presented here are not the best we can do. Other authors could compose better answers. Hopefully they will. Everyone is welcome to start from scratch with a much different approach.

Soon I will convene a workshop to evaluate this work-in-progress and agree on feedback. For more info, see TransformTheSystem.org. Everyone who comments on the website and leaves their email address will be invited to collaborate. (Respondents' email addresses will not be visible to the public or sold.)

Working together, let's help transform the system.

1: The System

What is "the system?" Does it have a central purpose?
If so, what is it? How is it structured and how does it operate?

Humans first evolved as hunter-gatherers in southern Africa. When Dutch migrants settled there, they reported that the native peoples were "always gay, always dancing and singing" and appeared to enjoy a life "without occupation or toil." A priest commented, "They are the happiest of men since they alone live in peace and freedom.... Their contempt for riches is in reality nothing but their hatred of work." According to those settlers, the indigenous people "seemed incapable of being pressed into labor."[25]

Farther north, hunter-gatherers, known as Bushmen, lived in an enormous desert that isolated them. Few people bothered to cross that desert. In the late twentieth century, anthropologists discovered a culture there much like what the early Dutch settlers had found closer to the coast. James Suzman describes the Bushmen as "the first small group of anatomically modern people who bind all of humankind into one family." He says our DNA gives all humanity an "inner hunter-gather."[26]

Reports on first contact with hunter-gatherer societies in other parts of the world are similar. The wikipedia says:

Hunter-gatherers tend to have an egalitarian social ethos....
Ethnographic data indicated that hunter-gatherers worked far
fewer hours and enjoyed more leisure than typical members of
industrial society, and they still ate well. Their "affluence"
came from the idea that they were satisfied with very little in
the material sense....[27]

Christopher Boehm studied data from forty-eight hunter-gatherer societies worldwide and concluded they practiced egalitarianism and usually did so very successfully. He found that the mechanisms they used to maintain equality included: public opinion; criticism and ridicule, and; extreme sanctions.[28] In so doing, they suppressed the domineering, bullying "alpha male" tendencies exhibited by our ape ancestors. They "self-domesticated" themselves. As humans breed animals to have certain characteristics, they bred human genes to foster cooperation.[29] After they learned that cooperation helped them survive, they selected mates who were cooperative.

Most humans were hunter-gatherers who lived in small bands, formed strong social bonds, were loyal to one another, took care of the vulnerable, respected their traditions, embraced their spirituality, and were committed to fairness. Those are basic human values. Suzman writes: "...the fifteen-hour working week was probably the norm for most of the estimated two-hundred-thousand-year history of biologically modern Homo sapiens."[30] They lived off the land and the animals they killed. Confident they could always get what they needed, they didn't store large quantities of food or seize nearby territories. When they lived in lush environments, they were generally peaceful toward nearby bands.

+++++

Then, after living as hunter-gatherers some 200,000 years, about 10,000 years ago, in different regions, climate change and population growth led to less abundant environments and humans began to settle in small towns, plant a variety of crops, raise animals, and store surplus food, while continuing to hunt and gather. Several thousand years later, they formed governments and built walls to protect themselves and their food. Those early states developed single-crop agriculture, which made it easier to tax subjects, and increasingly relied on trade. Taxes demonstrated submission to the government and were the price of protection.[31]

For the sake of greater security, many residents agreed to this arrangement. Living in larger, more complex communities enabled them to achieve goals they couldn't have otherwise. Their ability to cooperate and spread useful information efficiently was key to this transition. As societies became larger, the complex mental activities required to cooperate enlarged their brain, which enabled humans to evolve beyond our ape ancestors, both culturally and biologically. New religious institutions legitimized those new social structures, which perpetuated deeply ingrained cultural values concerning loyalty, respect for authority, worship of the sacred, fairness, and caring for one another.

Those early states often conquered nearby states. One motive was to strengthen their own power to minimize the risk of being invaded. Another motive was to bring home loot and slaves.

Those militaristic societies relied on a top-down structure dominated by male warriors. On the battlefield, decisions must be made quickly. Authority must be clear. Someone must be in charge. That dominate-or-submit pattern prevailed in tension with cooperative features that help hold societies together. Being able to count on everyone to fall in line when the next war broke out was critical.

The victors imposed taxable single-crop agriculture on their new subjects, which undermined self-sufficiency and created dependency on trade. The resulting sense of powerlessness fostered resentment, which drove conquered peoples to rebel and seek revenge. In that way, when they were victorious, a self-perpetuating pattern was established: expansion, domination, dependency, resentment, rebellion, revenge, victory; and, then again, expansion, domination, dependency, resentment, rebellion, revenge, victory, and on and on. (That cycle has persisted to this day.)

The new political and religious elites tried to eradicate the hunter-gatherer attachment to their leisurely lifestyles that conflicted with the long hours required by farm work. That effort was often unsuccessful. Many residents, including slaves, escaped from the confines of the walls that were meant to keep them in as well as keep out invaders.

+++++

Ever since the advent of large-scale agriculture, these patterns have persisted. Societies have centralized political power, established "upper" classes that dominate "lower" classes, and instilled certain traits in their subjects that help perpetuate those top-down structures. And in all developed societies, males have held the positions of highest power and discriminated against women.[32]

Early city-states grew into large regimes ruled by monarchs, such as kings and emperors, and far-flung empires. Those rulers passed on their wealth and power to their children — while sharing some of their privileges with upper-crust allies to buy loyalty and support.

But most of the world's population remained outside the boundaries of those agricultural empires. Hunter-gatherers and those who raised livestock rejected the drudgery of farming, sustained their cooperative traditions, were labeled "barbarians" or "savages," and resisted efforts to conquer them.

In Europe, during the reign of monarchs, living conditions and lifestyles for most people remained much the same from generation to generation and century to century — though the ruling elites grew increasingly wealthy. Most people retained traditional values including loyalty, fairness, mutual care, spirituality, and respect for authority. Then the emergence of capitalism spread wealth more broadly and fostered consumerism and individualism among the growing "middle class."[33]

Those newly enriched forces challenged the biological inheritance of wealth and power. To legitimize their challenge, they called on the egalitarian roots of their hunter-gatherer ancestors (often referred to as "the Golden Age"),[34] insisted all people are equal in the eyes of God, and demanded one person, one vote. This individualistic approach challenged traditional social bonds, obligations, and traditions.

Initially only property owners could vote. Over time, however, more people demanded to be treated as equals under the law and pushed for the right to vote. To protect their privileges, those with power shared some of their wealth and power. But they resisted calls for common ownership of all property and preserved society's essential top-down structure.[35]

In the British colonies, John Winthrop, a seventeenth-century leader of the Massachusetts Bay Colony, summed up a basic assumption for his newly forming community when he declared, "God Almightie in his most holy and wise providence hath soe disposed the Condition of mankind, as in all times some must be rich some poor, some high and eminent in power and dignitie; others mean and in subjection."[36]

Later, John Adams, the second President of the United States at the end of the eighteenth century, reinforced that point when he affirmed the "passion for distinction in the ranks and the order of society" and declared, "There must be one, indeed, who is the last and lowest of the human species."[37] Or, as the Tibetan Buddhist saying put it: "Envy toward the above, competitiveness toward the equal, and contempt toward the lower."[38] The balance between cooperation and domination established by hunter-gatherers was undermined.

+++++

Those individualistic beliefs remain deeply embedded. Families tell their children they must "get ahead" and can "be whatever you want to be."[39] The possibility of unlimited success is embedded as a realistic goal.[40] Churches preach the "prosperity gospel."[41] Schools teach students that only a few will really "win."[42] The media glorify celebrities.[43] Sports gurus instill that "winning is everything."[44] Doctors assume an air of authority that undermines self-care.[45] Paternalistic social-service agencies foster dependency on professionals.[46] People believe "someone must always be in charge."[47] Politicians focus on helping the "middle class," which reinforces the myth that upward mobility is the best way out of poverty.[48]

Each of those examples uses the same upward-mobility template: Climb the ladder, look down on those below, and envy those above. Dominate or submit is the prevailing message. Most people, driven by economic insecurity or the fear of "failure," build up their sense of self-worth by relentlessly comparing themselves to others. As civilizations developed, domineering spread throughout society — in families, schools, religious institutions, workplaces, governments, and elsewhere. People learned to spend most of their time either dominating or submitting.

America celebrates wealth. Overwhelming majorities of Americans "admire people who get rich by working hard."[49] Most Americans believe "the rich deserve their wealth."[50] In 2012 only 48% believed the inequality gap was a problem. Andrew Kohut, president of the Pew Research Center wrote: "People don't necessarily want to take money from the wealthy; they just want a better chance to get rich themselves." "Being wealthy" and "successful in a career" are important goals for most Americans.[51]

Still, trusting, cooperative cultures stayed alive. Though they were isolated from each other, in every large society, humans passed on memories of the early "Golden Age" or "Garden of Eden" — initially through oral histories and later in literature. Many families and small communities —

whether religious, utopian, political, or economic — sustained trusting, egalitarian, peaceful values with a wide variety of counter cultures that nurtured a fundamentally different society. And with some success, grassroots forces have fought tooth-and-nail to push for more compassion, cooperation, democracy, economic security, peace, and racial and social justice. In some respects, America is shifting toward more compassion, cooperation, trust and respect.

But those changes have provoked a backlash from forces invested in division and domination. Individuals with relatively more power inflame fear to serve their own self-interest. In the primal tension between cooperation and domination, divisive instincts often take over.

+++++

As with the environment and the human body, a system is a self-perpetuating web of relationships between interdependent elements that reinforce one another to establish balance and continuity.[52] A system is greater than the sum of its parts.[53] With systems, cause-and-effect is not linear as is the pain that results when we hit a thumb with a hammer. Rather, many factors influence one another and interact to cause events.[54] To understand a system, you must understand its whole web.[55] A system operates **as if** it were a concrete entity with a mind of its own.[56] That's why we talk about families and organizations as unified, distinct units. As summed up by Stanford Beers, "The purpose of a system is what it does."[57] The environment perpetuates evolution; the human body sustains life; families raise children. Societies are stable over time because they are coherent social systems.[58]

Today, our institutions, our culture, and we ourselves as individuals are woven together into a self-perpetuating global social system, the System. The primary purpose of the System is to enable individuals to gain more status, wealth, and power over others. Its driving force is the effort to climb one social ladder or another. The resulting mixture of top-down domination and widespread consumerism is the System as we know it. As the world has been Americanized, the System has become global.[59]

In the United States, as more people achieved the right to vote, the System gained sufficient loyalty to sustain itself by expanding opportunities for upward mobility. It has offered more people more privileges, especially the ability to buy new consumer products. America has always been torn between trust and fear. But our social system has primarily relied on fear and domination.

Those with the power to determine who can move up a ladder weigh various factors in making their decisions. Those factors are often arbitrary. Examples include race, gender, family pedigree, age, "attractiveness," cultural tastes, political beliefs, accent, social etiquette, submissiveness, capacity for linear thinking, and willingness to work overtime.[60]

Individuals hold different positions on different ladders. We may submit at work and dominate at home. We may feel our race is superior to others. We may look down on those with more education, or envy those with more. But we spend most of our time either dominating or submitting. We get so caught up in one of our identities we don't identify strongly as a member of the human family.

In one form or another, rankism permeates society. Robert Fuller, who coined the term, says rankism is "an assertion of superiority" and "is a residue of predation" that derives from our history of preying on others and serves to:

> *demean, marginalize, and disenfranchise.... We "do" rankism to institutionalize and normalize predation.... We practice rankism to put ourselves in a position to prey on others...and more safely exploit them in future. Or, so they will not compete with us. Or, simply to feel superior.... Fixing the game is the real reason for rankism. If we can handicap or eliminate the competition, we improve our*

chances of coming away with the spoils.... We've kept it a secret because it diminishes our achievement to admit the game was rigged in our favor.[61]

Clearly everyone is not equal in every way. Some have certain skills that others do not. But rankism's key message is that certain people are **essentially** superior, as a basic condition of their being. That superiority supposedly entitles them to special treatment in the eyes of the law and society at large.

Rankism may have served a necessary evolutionary purpose. Those habits are useful in certain situations. But the question is whether we need to learn how to set aside those habits in situations that call for egalitarian cooperation.[62] Can we restore a balance between trust (which leads to love and cooperation) and fear (which leads to anger and domination), and live up to America's highest ideals?

2: Reinforcing the System

How do we, as individuals and with our organizations, reinforce the system?

Each day, with the items we buy, the taxes we pay, the way we treat other people, and countless other ways, we strengthen the System.

Egalitarian relationships are rooted in trust, mutual respect, and compassion. Everyone gives and receives more-or-less equally. We care about each other. We listen carefully and reveal ourselves. When we disagree, we try to understand the other. We want to learn from others and ask questions to increase our understanding of their perspective. One-on-one conversations are real dialogs. In group conversations, when we've been doing most of the talking, we give space to those who've been quieter.

In today's America, those egalitarian patterns are not the norm. Most Americans often demonstrate kindness, but self-centeredness prevails. One or two individuals monopolize most group discussions. Conversations are typically a series of monologues: telling stories about the past, gossiping, lecturing. Active listening is rare.[63] "Yes, the same thing happened to me" followed by the respondent's own story about himself seems to be the most frequent form of empathy. College students today are about forty percent less empathetic than twenty or thirty years ago.[64] Taller people are more likely to be dominant. Talking loudly, interrupting, and talking longer and faster are signs of dominance. Nonverbal messages such as leaning forward, using gestures, and touching others physically also indicate dominance.[65] Submissive people prefer to interact with dominant people, and dominant people prefer to interact with submissive people.[66] In my taxi, when I'd ask a male-female couple in the back seat a question, the male almost always answered. Without exception, every rented two-seat bicycle I've seen has been driven by the man, not the woman.

Rankism affects us at our core and shapes our identity. We constantly score ourselves on one scale or another and compare ourselves to others. We generally don't treat others as individuals who are equal in the eyes of God, but rather assume someone will be King of the Hill. As Stanley declared in *A Streetcar Named Desire*, husbands have traditionally believed "I am the King around here, so don't forget it!"[67] The title of the 1950s sitcom "Father Knows Best" has been a common message that persists. *The New York Times* reports:

> *The sociologists Joanna Pepin and David Cotter find that the proportion of young people holding egalitarian views about gender relationships rose steadily from 1977 to the mid-1990s but has fallen since. In 1994, only 42 percent of high school seniors agreed that the best family was one where the man was the main income earner and the woman took care of the home. But in 2014, 58 percent of seniors said they preferred that arrangement.*[68]

Climbing a ladder of success is the focus of life for most Americans. When meeting someone new, one of the first questions asked is: "What work do you do?" The answer influences how people react — whether they feel equal, superior, or inferior.

The American Dream promises that hard work will lead to upward mobility, prosperity, and social status. Faith in that Dream fosters the belief that those who don't succeed are deficient in some fundamental way.[69] Lack of success indicates moral failure. Those higher up look down on those below and are domineering when they interact with them. And those lower down tend to worship those higher up — unless they're resentful and rebel.

To climb ladders, children, students, and workers traditionally submit to parents, teachers, and bosses. Those dominant-submissive relationships are often rational. It may be necessary to keep a job, for instance. When decisions must be made quickly, someone must have the authority to make it. One recent study found that most marriages included a dominant partner (24% of whom were women) and concluded that such arrangements are a practical way to minimize time-consuming conflict.[70] All that can make sense for some partners. Power differences are often understandable.

But when dominate-or-submit becomes a habit that carries over throughout life it can be problematic, as reflected in the title of a large conference convened by the Esalen Institute, the fountainhead of the human potential movement, in the 1970s: "Spiritual and Therapeutic Tyranny: The Willingness to Submit."[71]

The dominate-or-submit habit leads to assumptions that:

- Someone must always be in charge.
- Leaders set the vision for organizations and define what can be discussed.
- Leadership is defined as the ability to mobilize followers.

But many social relationships are most fruitful when participants relate as equals. Given society's conditioning and the fact that most people spend most of their time in dominant-submissive relationships, which becomes a habit, such equality can be difficult to sustain.

Dominate-or-submit habits also carry over into how people treat members of other groups. Messages from early childhood produce subconscious bias that favors ingroups and discriminates against outgroups.[72] As a result, we see:

- Lighter-skinned people of color are treated differently than those who are darker-skinned.[73]
- Coastal elites are condescending toward "flyover country."[74]
- Rural residents blame "city slickers" for their problems.[75]

- To protect their job or advance their career, women have submitted to sexual harassment.[76]
- With their paternalism, social service organizations disempower clients.[77]
- People who hold the power to punish, such as police, prison guards, and military personnel, often abuse their power, especially if it conforms to expectations from above.[78]
- America assumes it must "lead" the world.[79]

Some of those patterns of interpersonal and intergroup domination are changing. Many families are more egalitarian. The movement against sexual harassment is encouraging women to be less submissive and teaching men to be less domineering. Many businesses are more horizontal.[80] And racism, sexism, homophobia and other forms of oppression may be slowly diminishing, somewhat.

But schools are becoming more authoritarian.[81] Our politics are becoming more judgmental. And at school, work, and home Americans generally still either dominate or submit more often than they engage in equal relationships.

The rhetoric of meritocracy — the claim that individuals are rewarded based on ability rather than class privilege — is used to justify these patterns. But in fact, wealth, status, and power are largely inherited; families pass on their advantages to their children. Most adults are roughly in the same socioeconomic class as their parents. The social inheritance of wealth and power has replaced biological inheritance.[82]

The System has seduced almost everyone into pursuing upward mobility. Even non-materialistic social workers and political activists engage in ego-driven power games. The personal identities of individuals depend on their rank. Mutual respect among collaborators who treat one another as equals takes a back seat to gaining status and power.

+++++

The System rationalizes oppression by promoting individualism — the doctrine that the interests of the individual are most important. The mantra of the modern age is "What's in it for me?" The ego is king. Even children become extensions of their parents' ego, to be molded in their parents' image. The result is growing personal isolation.

One recent study asked participants to list the names of people with whom they had discussed "important matters" over the previous six months. About fifty percent listed only one name. The average number of such confidantes had decreased from three to two over the previous twenty-five years.[83] The number of people who report feeling lonely has increased from twenty to forty percent since the 1980s.[84] Almost half of all meals are eaten alone.[85] The average American now spends less than four minutes a day — twenty-four hours a year — participating in organized social events.[86] Social isolation greatly increases the odds for getting sick, suffering cognitive deficits, or dying prematurely.[87] And as isolation undermines the habit of collaborating with neighbors to solve problems, that social environment, as Sam Quinones wrote, creates "the natural habitat not just of heroin but of that next young killer now planning to roam a school corridor."[88]

This pattern is aggravated by mobile phones. The Internet helps people connect in certain ways, but it also encourages us to drift apart into silos. People spend more time writing messages than reading messages from others. That pattern carries over into real life. They spend so much time looking at screens they lose the satisfaction of simultaneous shared experience and fail to develop the social skills needed to resolve conflict.[89] Soulful, mutual dialogue — speaking spontaneously from the heart with one's whole being — is becoming rarer. People get stuck on a superficial level of self-awareness and self-interest.

When I asked Rhonda Magee about the price we must pay to trust each other, as James Baldwin envisioned, and suggested it involves dissolving our identity as a "superior" person who should dominate, she commented:

> Yes. So true. I think another trap is thinking that all of the work is personal, to be seen through an individualism lens. Our fears are shaped in part by environments in which we live, by systemic vulnerabilities that reinforce separation and the sense of needing to live in a defended way. This kind of vulnerability is easier to write about that to live. Being in connected community helps, but so often these are grounded in identity.... hence the enormity of the challenges we face.[90]

A common form of individualism is scapegoating, which operates in relationships, families, the workplace, and society at large. Looking for someone to blame is widespread. But blaming any one factor in a system is a diversion, a simplification, a way to avoid confronting complexity. In any system, causes are interwoven and influence one another. With social systems, the main problem is not any one individual or any one group; it's the system.

We can hold specific individuals accountable for specific actions. We might even punish them. But it's wrong to exaggerate their responsibility. To do so neglects the importance of other factors, including our own individual responsibility for helping to perpetuate the System. Everyone's a pawn. Even top-level administrators are easily replaced.

When it's fueled by anger, scapegoating leads to demonizing. Opponents become enemies. Judgments become judgmental. We project onto them weaknesses that we hold within ourselves but fail to face. Rather than acknowledge our own responsibility, we criticize others harshly and place excessive blame on their shoulders.

The scapegoat becomes a devil we must defeat by any means necessary. Winning becomes everything. The end justifies the means. An enemy of our enemy is a friend. We divide the world into good guys and bad guys. We fail to be the change we seek.

Political activists are prone to blame the President, the other political party, Wall Street, "liberal elites," "irredeemable deplorables," "Washington," or other handy targets. People who are frustrated take out their anger on handy punching bags, inflame threats, and amplify fears.

Judgmental personal attacks reinforce the System. They neglect the social context, overlook the fact that everyone is a victim, and exaggerate the responsibility of individuals. Scapegoating diverts energy from the pursuit of meaningful structural reforms and undermines the unity needed for positive, proactive change. Crushing individuals will not transform the System.

+++++

Following the fall of the Soviet Union, in his 1990 Nobel Prize for Literature lecture Octavio Paz warned:

> ...The collapse of Utopian schemes has left a great void... For the first time in history mankind lives in a sort of spiritual wilderness... It is a dangerous experience.... Men could then become possessed once more by ancient religious fury or by fanatical nationalism. It would be terrible if the fall of the abstract idol of ideology were to foreshadow the resurrection of the buried passions of tribes, sects and churches. The signs, unfortunately, are disturbing.[91]

His fears have been realized. The world is fragmenting. Brutal civil wars, ethnic cleansing, anti-immigrant hysteria, racism, and military skirmishes are worsening. One is led to ask: In struggles like those between Iran and Saudi Arabia, and Israel and Palestine, why does the United States so often take sides in ways that worsen the situation? Why can't the U.S. adopt a neutral stance and try to mediate reconciliation? An "America First" foreign policy, which echoes America's "Me First" culture, aggravates fragmentation, undermines cooperation between nations, and inflames the "fanatical nationalism" Paz warned about.

It seems likely that at least one reason why elected officials have chosen this course is that foreign crises distract attention from problems at home. The "war on terror," which is greatly disproportionate to the threat that terrorism poses to the United States, may be the perfect war to distract attention from domestic problems. There's nothing like a war to strengthen the standing of a President. And it's never-ending because it creates more terrorists than it kills. When will the United States stop being so influenced by domestic political calculations and stop acting like the world's policeman?

Fragmentation is happening within the United States as well. After World War Two, corporations, labor unions, and the federal government agreed on a "Social Contract." Businesses accepted unions and increased wages, which boosted the economy. For twenty-five years, incomes at every level increased at about the same rate. In addition, activists gained regulations to protect consumers and the environment by imposing limits on businesses. And Democrats and Republicans often compromised on legislation. Most Republicans, for example, voted for civil rights legislation in the 1960s. To a considerable degree, America was united.

Then, in the early 1970s, many corporate elites appeared to get nervous about the future. One source of concern was that in the 694 days between January 11, 1973 and December 6, 1974, stocks lost over forty-five percent of their value. Faced with numerous threats like that, many wealthy elites apparently decided to tear up the Social Contract and make as much money as they could as quickly as they could.[92] As a result, the share of the nation's net personal wealth owned by the richest 0.1 percent increased from seven percent in 1979 to twenty-two percent in 2012.[93]

During those years, the Democratic Party largely helped the Republicans establish those new economic policies. The Republicans would stake out an extreme position, and the Democrats would show they were different by adopting a somewhat less extreme position. But the Republicans, who became increasingly radical, had the momentum.

As the country becomes ever more polarized, rank-and-file Democrats and Republicans now tend to support almost anything their leaders advocate. Rabid Republicans, rabid Democrats, religious and political sects, ultra-nationalists, white supremacists, and other "tribes" have all become firmly rooted in their dogmas.

Powerful forces are reducing human lives to disposable tools. People are competing more fiercely in an unpredictable world. Though our world is increasingly interdependent, "rugged individuals" deny their dependence on others. Driven in large part by economic insecurities and resentments, and an aggressive, militaristic foreign policy, those forces threaten to tear the world apart.

3: A New Mission

Would a transformed society have a new mission?
If so, what should it be?

Society needs an agreed-on mission to maintain stability. Otherwise the social fabric tears apart. In the Preamble to its Constitution, the United States declares:

We the People of the United States, in Order to form a more perfect Union, establish Justice, insure domestic Tranquility, provide for the common defence, promote the general Welfare, and secure the Blessings of Liberty to ourselves and our Posterity, do ordain and establish this Constitution for the United States of America.[94]

That's a good statement, but it applies only to the government. A new purpose for society-as-a-whole could help us overcome our weaknesses, enhance our strengths, live up to our ideals more fully, and add to our valuable traditions. Toward that end this draft declaration suggests that Americans adopt the following mission:

To help transform our nation into a compassionate community dedicated to the common good of all humanity, our own people, the environment, and life itself.

If residents of other countries adopt the same mission for their country, our nations will be better able to cooperate, serve that shared purpose, and help transform the System.

To nurture compassionate communities, we must commit to self-development, which depends on communal support. Even hermits need community. The Lone Ranger is a myth. Strong individuals need strong communities, and strong communities need strong individuals. Even if we become more self-reliant as we mature, we still rely on others. Companionship, physical sustenance, and moral support continue to be important. Americans often try to deny it, but individuals are interdependent — entangled in multiple webs, social and environmental.

In addition to their individual identity, humans hold multiple other identities, such as a member of a family, community, city, state, and nation. When we go deep within, however, we connect with the foundation of all life and experience what we have in common with all humanity. We identify as members of the human family. In doing so, we don't totally drop the multiple roles society has embedded in us, but we don't concede the last word to society. We don't reduce ourselves or others to labels. At least from time to time, we can:

- recognize our shared humanity and create new identities;
- affirm that we're human, good enough, and can still be better;
- be true to who we really are and liberate our inner hunter-gatherer;
- remember that everyone is a victim of the System;
- commit to transform the System, as well as more fully realize our potential as individuals;
- aim to reform the structure and character of our social system and make our society and ourselves more caring, just and democratic;
- love ourselves as we love others;
- avoid both selfishness and self-sacrifice.

We can recognize universal human needs and accept our moral obligation to attend to those needs. As Simone Weil declared, "There is something sacred in every human being, but it is not their person. It is this human being; no more and no less."[95]

Being grounded in the universal life force helps us trust that Life will take care of herself. Fear's valuable when the perceived threat is real. But irrational fear is deadly. We need to measure threats accurately and know who we can trust and how we can trust them.

Irrational trust, however, is blind romanticism. Rational trust, on the other hand, enables us to appreciate non-material or spiritual realities, be in harmony with nature, and be awestruck by beauty when we encounter it. We're motivated by a desire to relieve suffering and work with others to reduce injustice. We accept the restrained use of police power to hold back those who want to violate the rights of others. We accept legitimate authority that controls excessive chaos by imposing some degree of order. We accept taxation. We accept the need for a division of labor that delegates to certain individuals the responsibility and power to make certain decisions in a compassionate manner, while maximizing collaboration.

Rational trust leads to:

- acceptance of others as individuals with equal essential worth;
- a sense of community with all humanity;
- collaboration with partners;
- relating to others fully and mutually;
- trying to understand and improve the world;
- a determination to control the alpha-male instinct to dominate that we inherited from our ape ancestors.

A balance that integrates rational trust and rational fear leads to a higher, more evolved unity. It involves compassionate power with, not power over. Maintaining that balance requires critical self-examination.

The comic strip character Pogo said, "We have met the enemy and it is us."[96] He had a point. Each of us shares responsibility for the state of the world. To deal with rankism, we must change ourselves as well as society.

Claudia Horwitz wrote:

Have we given in to the darker side of our nature in some unconscious way that we're not totally aware of? Have we been complicit? Do we really want to do that?... There are ancestral, cultural, and political legacies that survive and thrive because they're not interrupted with some kind of searing reflective lens.[97]

Most Americans would like to be less judgmental and more compassionate. They'd like to love their "enemies." They want to engage with others as equals. They know that trying to relieve suffering can be rewarding. When they think deeply about it, Americans realize:

- The individual and the community are interwoven. What affects one individual affects every individual.
- What serves the individual serves the community, and what serves the community serves the individual.
- The Earth *is* a spaceship and yes, all humanity is in this together.
- There's no irreconcilable conflict between self-interest and community-interest, though there's often a tension.

Building an effective compassionate, transformative movement will require activists to liberate those innate instincts.

For various reasons, however, most people are not committed to ongoing self-improvement. Instead, they reflect one or more of the following characteristics. They:

- fail to acknowledge mistakes and resolve not to repeat them.
- aren't ready to pay the price required for self-development.
- seem to believe they pretty much have it all together, have matured as much as they can, and are coping well enough.
- are afraid to fail.
- believe that being widely recognized as very successful is terribly important.
- are rooted in an identity that is based on how well they climb social ladders.

- proceed with lives of quiet or not-so-quiet desperation.
- find a comfort zone and choose to stick with it.
- submit to some people, dominate others, and relate to few as equals.
- respect members of their "tribe" and demean "the other," which gives their life some meaning.
- follow leaders because when they do so they have fewer decisions to make.
- choose to avoid challenging top-down structures because prospects for success are often dim and can lead to frustrating failure, cause conflict, or subject rebels to punishment.

The reluctance to engage in self-improvement is even more true of political activists who focus on the outer world. The pressure to stop injustice and relieve suffering is enormous. Taking a break to engage in self-examination can seem like self-indulgent navel-gazing; there's no time to waste. The prevailing attitude is: "We have the answer. Join us, and we'll impose it on those who don't understand."

But that outer-focused activism reinforces the System, which many activists say they want to reform. The extreme focus on measurable, written policies reinforces materialism, the belief that only physical factors matter. And focusing on crushing enemies helps to divide and conquer. Potential recruits are turned off by preaching, strident speeches, fear-mongering, scapegoating, ad hominem attacks, hate, uncontrolled anger, verbal violence that nurtures physical violence, and the failure to engage others in problem-solving collaboration, negotiation and compromise. Overcoming those tendencies isn't easy.

The first step is to commit, really commit, to serve the common good of all humanity as well as one's own people, the environment, and life itself — as affirmed in the mission statement proposed here. A commitment to that mission requires a dedication to self-improvement. Constantly remind yourself: I am not the point. The local is global. The global is local. The personal is political. The political is personal. Connect the dots. Plant seeds. Understand and describe your efforts as one step toward global transformation. Place your work within the context of the Big Picture. Stay focused on the mission. Transforming the world into a compassionate community of individuals who respect one another will require widespread, ongoing self-development, egalitarianism, collaborative leadership, and love.

+++++

Compassionate activists follow reality wherever it leads them. Being pragmatic idealists, they judge an action by its results, by whether it relieves suffering, not whether it serves some abstract cause. They avoid ideology, visionary theorizing that worships abstractions divorced from reality.

Ideologues idolize certain words as if they hold magical powers. They automatically oppose, or support, a proposal based not on its practical impact, but on whether it advances their ideology.

For example, ideologues may oppose or support a proposal simply on whether or not it enhances the role of "the government." They want to "make a point." Those who are "anti-government" may oppose legislation to discourage similar legislation in the future, thereby preventing a potential "slippery slope." And those who are "pro-government" may support the same legislation to build momentum *for* the government. Neither side really evaluates the merits of each case.

Another example are capitalists who say a "free market" uninhibited by any governmental interference would produce enormous prosperity. But there never has been a totally free market and there never will be. Governments have always boosted certain interests over others, and they always will, as they should. And large corporations have undermined free markets by creating monopolies. Only the government can bust up monopolies.

The notion of the self-made businessman is nonsense. Without relying on the history of accumulated knowledge developed by others, the backing of the government, other forms of social support, and (usually) good luck, successful entrepreneurs couldn't accomplish anything. Yet society gives credit to those who rise to the top and blame those who do not. Special contempt is reserved for those at the bottom. Victims of natural disasters receive aid, but victims of our ongoing social disaster aren't offered living-wage job opportunities. Nevertheless, some people automatically oppose any government "interference." They always want to make their abstract point, rather than address concrete pros and cons. They are ideologues.

Likewise, "anti-capitalists" typically don't explain how they would abolish capitalism. Post-capitalism, would a family be able to open a corner grocery and set its own prices? Would another David Packard be able to start a new business in his garage and grow it into a billion-dollar company? Would worker-owned cooperatives be able to borrow capital from banks and set prices on their products? Would cab drivers be private workers? Would remarkably successful authors and musicians be able to sell an unlimited number of their products? Would we keep the stock market? The abolition of capitalism could lead to a No answer on all those questions, yet most anti-capitalists attack capitalism without answering such questions. The word "capitalism" serves as an anti-icon they demonize in their use of empty, abstract rhetoric. Those anti-capitalists are also ideologues.

Any modern economy is sure to be a mixed economy, a blend of private enterprise, publicly owned services, and government regulation. The question is what kind of mix there will be — where to employ one method and where to employ another, and how. Ideology doesn't answer that question.

There are many other ideologues, all of them recognizable by their use of absolute language and black-and-white thinking. Examples include:

- those who oppose, or support, abortion in **all** circumstances;
- those who oppose **all** economic growth, even if it involves only renewable products and green energy;
- those who will **only** support single-payer health insurance, which is but one path to universal coverage;
- Democrats who **always** refuse to collaborate with Republicans, and vice versa;
- those who oppose **any** incremental legislative victories because such reforms supposedly always reinforce the System;
- those who oppose **any** tax increase;
- those who oppose **all** foreign aid.

With all these groups, the pattern is consistent. Ideologues lock into an idea that is represented by a word or phrase, and they worship those words like a religious icon or doctrine that is repeated like a broken record. As a result, they have little regard for the complexities of reality or any willingness to evaluate options.

The mission statement for our society proposed here aims to avoid those ideological traps by only affirming fundamental values and key principles and leaving it to a genuine democratic process to concretely implement those values and principles. Cultivating compassionate community requires that kind of free-wheeling, open-ended process.

The System deeply embeds counter-productive habits, values, and personality traits. Subject to relentless dehumanization, we're inflamed by reality-distorting fears that reinforce the System with top-down domination.

But the System is torn. It also includes some bottom-up democracy, and especially in our private lives and small communities, Americans have sustained trust, love and cooperation. The mission statement proposed here aims to suppress the System's tendency toward top-down power so that feature will operate only when really needed. Then we can move toward transforming our nation into a compassionate community dedicated to the common good of all humanity, our own people, the environment, and life itself.

4: A Transformed Society

How would a transformed society be organized?
What would it look like?

The social change proposed in this draft declaration is *systemic transformation*. To transform means "to change in composition or structure, to change the outward form or appearance of, or to change in character or condition." Transforming America into a compassionate and fair society will require new social structures that facilitate democracy, enhance equality, promote dignity for all, and help everyone be all they can be.

One such structural reform is to transform the job market as a step toward economic security for all. The United States has more than enough money to assure that every worker can find a good living-wage job. When that goal is achieved, unemployment offices could refer workers to one of those jobs, whether private or public.

The need for more public-service jobs is compelling. The lack of quality services to meet human needs is enormous. Underfunded programs include: child care; preschool centers; nursing homes; in-home caregiving; park and recreation programs; teacher's aides; substance-abuse programs; neighborhood centers; cultural centers, and; after-school programs. There's also a pressing need to clean up and protect the environment.

A caring economy would assure essential services from the cradle to the grave. Theoretically, a truly compassionate society could meet those needs informally, in families and communities. But in the modern world, public funding for paid human services is essential. The private sector will never meet the need. Clients often don't have enough income to generate profits for providers.

Twenty million working-age Americans not in college are unemployed. With access to on-the-job training, many of those Americans could address unmet needs.

We're not talking about guaranteed jobs or a guaranteed income. We're talking about a living-wage job *opportunity*. Able working-age adults would be required to work to get public funding, and disabled workers would work according to their ability. Taxpayers don't want their money going to people who refuse to work, and indefinite handouts are morally questionable. But a plurality of Americans supports a federal job guarantee. It's not a radical idea.

A new federal bureaucracy would not be necessary. A national jobs trust fund could distribute money to local governments for public-service jobs. Wealthy individuals could make tax-deductible donations to that fund and the federal government could contribute to it with revenue sharing as needed to assure living-wage job opportunities. Local governments would either hire workers themselves or distribute funds to nonprofit organizations. The federal government would raise the needed funds from various sources.

The richest one percent currently pays only thirty-three percent of their income in federal taxes. If they paid forty-five percent instead, that higher rate would generate about $300 billion a year in new federal revenue, which could pay for nine million $15 per hour jobs — and those taxpayers would still have an average of at least one million dollars in annual after-tax income.[98]

Money can be raised in other ways as well. To cite just two examples: putting more people to work would boost the economy, which would generate additional tax revenue, and; large sums could be freed up by finding waste in the $600 billion military budget (legislators often give the military more money than they request to help themselves get re-elected by creating local jobs).

Other methods could also help ensure economic security:

- provide paid vacations and steadily reduce the workweek, which would boost employment by spreading the workload over a larger workforce;
- rebuild family farms, which would revive rural economies;
- increasing the number of worker-owned businesses, which would reduce the number of businesses moving to other countries;
- enable anyone to buy into Medicare health insurance;
- greatly increase funding for non-profit affordable housing.

The bottom line is that a truly compassionate society would provide everyone with a decent opportunity to meet their basic needs — with publicly funded services when needed. Some people would still fail to take advantage of those opportunities. But they would be few in number and could receive support privately from friends, relatives, and non-profit organizations.

As James Suzman noted, "The kind of egalitarianism practiced by hunter-gatherers was ... the outcome of people acting in their own self-interest.... Everyone got their fair share."[99] The same sentiment applies to contemporary America. Ensuring a foundation of economic security for everyone is not only a moral imperative. It would benefit the entire society.

Economic security would nurture non-material values. If people trusted that they would always be able to make ends meet, they could more easily enjoy their leisure time, be with their families, become more fully human, engage in self-improvement and ongoing education, help create a more compassionate society, and participate in communal life, including political action.

People could still climb a social ladder if they wanted to, but they wouldn't have to in order to live decently. The upward-mobility template would lose some of its power. Dog-eat-dog hyper-competition would become less prevalent. As more people liberated their inner hunter-gatherer, the positive effects would ripple throughout society.

So long as people remain focused on protecting their status or trying to hit a jackpot in the casino economy, they won't be free — and there will be little hope for social transformation. Universal economic security would help make society more democratic and egalitarian.

So long as some children live in poverty, they're not equal. Our society doesn't allow all, or most, poor children to "make it" by means of hard work and merit because the number of people needing work exceeds the number of living-wage jobs. And the human costs inflicted by poverty can last a lifetime. No child should have to grow up in poverty because their parents can't find a living-wage job.

Many liberals want to clean up the System by eliminating unfair discrimination and providing compensatory education and social support to poor youth. They talk about strengthening the middle class with upward mobility. But even if black and brown poor people had an equal opportunity with whites to climb out of poverty, children growing up poor would still suffer.

Helping some Americans move up the economic ladder is no great victory if most Americans barely hold on and many are stuck in extreme poverty or homelessness. But politicians prefer to talk about mobility rather than creating jobs.

Universal economic security would also help erode the deep-seated racism that's aggravated by widespread resentment about unfair living conditions. As the top one percent takes more of the nation's income for itself, growing inequality and economic hard times inflame racism and lead many white Americans to direct their anger at people of color. Study after study show that racism is still a serious problem in the United States. Personal reports reinforce those findings. But it's often not easy for whites to face their racism. Gut reactions and unconscious bias are hard to acknowledge.[100] If all Americans trusted they'd always be able to make ends meet in a transformed society, they could more easily admit mistakes, learn from them, and move beyond racism.

In the political arena, structural reforms that could give people more voice in shaping their daily life include:

- Get rid of Big Money in politics and strengthen "one person, one vote" by overturning *Citizens United*, the 2010 Supreme Court ruling that authorized unlimited spending by wealthy individuals to influence political campaigns and legislation.[101] Free speech can legitimately be restricted when it interferes with the rights of others, and allowing the super-rich to spend millions on political speech weakens democracy by undermining the power of those who are not wealthy.

- Build more democratic activist organizations. When members select their leaders and have a voice in shaping policy, they're more likely to sense ownership and support it actively. Smaller groups can try to reach unanimous consensus on decisions and use a super-majority, such as 80%, if necessary. When large minorities object to a proposal they usually have a point and ignoring them often leads to splintering, but always requiring unanimous consensus can be unwieldy. Large organizations can also use a super-majority.

- Form a grassroots "Purple Alliance" that pushes for positive changes in national policy that are supported by a majority of Republicans, Independents, and Democrats. That alliance could focus on one such "crossover" priority at a time and stick with it until it is resolved. Local teams could engage in nonviolent direct action when needed to build support for that measure. A deliberate nationwide planning process, similar to those that have been convened by Adam Kahane and his Reos Partners, could be used to develop the structure for that alliance.

- Persuade or require Congresspersons and Senators to hold orderly monthly forums streamed live — at the same time each month — to enable *randomly selected* constituents to engage in dialog with those officials or their chiefs of staff. Those community dialogues would be carefully structured with a neutral moderator to assure that the officials do not dominate. Constituents could use their time to ask questions or make comments. Community organizations could distribute literature at these lively civic gatherings.
- Transform one of the current political parties into a bottom-up activist organization that engages in face-to-face precinct-based community building and fights for its national platform *year-round* — or create a new one that does. That party could commit itself to focusing on proposed changes in national policy that are supported by majorities of Republicans, Independents, and Democrats — and help form a Purple Alliance with the same commitment. If and when one of its representatives repeatedly failed to adequately support the party's national campaign, it could support a challenger in the next primary.
- Federal funding for a non-profit corporation to conduct regular community dialogs with randomly selected Americans, using "deliberative polling," to formulate advice to Washington on key issues.[102] These events, televised on C-SPAN, could be a way to increase public awareness and help form solutions. A random, representative sample of the public would be recruited to participate. Prior to the event, a panel of experts would provide participants balanced briefing materials on the issue. Participants would then be randomly assigned to small groups with trained moderators to discuss the issue and develop questions to present to a panel of experts and policymakers. The event would conclude with

participants completing a questionnaire about their opinions on the issue. The results would be circulated to the public, Congress, and the President.

- In school, rely less on preparing for tests and the one-way transmission of information by teachers and instead create more opportunities for self-directed and peer learning based on real partnerships between students, parents and administrators.
- Encourage and support public-benefit corporations that serve the public interest as well as earn a profit.
- Provide tax breaks, low-interest loans, and technical assistance for worker-owned businesses.
- Stop the federal government from helping businesses bust unions, but rather support unionization so workers can benefit more when businesses prosper.
- Expand restorative justice programs, which bring victims, offenders and community members together to repair the harm caused by crime.[103]
- Assure that jails and prisons honor the humanity of those who are restrained and support their self-development.
- Revive rural communities by supporting green businesses and backing family farms.

In foreign policy, facing no threat of being conquered, America could help put a stop to the cycle of domination, resistance, retaliation, and revenge that began with the early city-states in the Middle East several thousand years ago. Such a course could lead to greater acceptance of the fact that win-win solutions are the only viable path forward. True patriots, in honor of America's fight for independence, should reject efforts to dominate other countries.

Strong nation states are essential to restrain powerful, global corporate and financial forces. Because our world has become increasingly interdependent, nations need to cooperate to maintain their independence. No nation can seek its own ends unilaterally, and no global governing elite can run the whole world.

Every day, the need for a global commitment to serve the common good of the entire Earth community is ever more urgent. Its motto should be: "The more you thrive, the more we thrive!" The United States should help other countries prosper, stop trying to dominate the world, accept our limits, apologize for our mistakes, resolve not to repeat them, and form real partnerships with other countries. We should:

- focus on alliances with countries that work to advance values we embrace, including human rights, equal treatment under the law, the rights of minorities, and democracy;
- stop taking sides so quickly in conflicts between and within countries and help the United Nations mediate when feasible;
- support national self-determination and refrain from interfering in the internal affairs or other nations;
- stop selling weapons to authoritarian countries.

In the social arena, structural reforms need to include:

- include anti-bullying, nonviolent communication, active listening, and peer counseling education in our schools;
- throughout society expand the use of conflict resolution methods to facilitate the peaceful ending of conflict;[104]
- establish effective mechanisms for reporting, investigating, correcting, and if necessary punishing sexual harassment;
- in social-service agencies, support structures that give clients a collective voice about how those agencies operate;
- in small supportive groups, members regularly support one another in their self-development and set aside time to provide that support;

- create model alternative institutions such as farmers' markets and cultural centers;
- build structures in non-profit organizations that more fully empower their members;
- In private businesses, expand the use of holacracy, which is:

a self-management practice for running purpose-driven, responsive companies. By empowering people to make meaningful decisions and drive change, the Holacracy practice unleashes your organization's untapped power to pursue its purpose in the world. [105]

- promote non-profit social entrepreneurs who address social, cultural, and environmental issues.[106]

In addition to those structural reforms, we Americans need to improve how we relate to one another informally. While accepting that in some situations domination and submission is justified or necessary, we can avoid allowing those patterns to become habits that carry over into situations where relating to others as equals is called for.

Most people have prejudicial gut reactions, but they need not allow those reactions to shape their behavior. Factors that prompt such reactions include skin color, gender, sexual preference, age, disability, level of education, appearance, social status, accent, job, political and religious opinions, and place of residence. There seems to be an unlimited number of ways that humans forget that we are all created equal and are fundamentally invested with equal worth. But we can learn to set aside those prejudices, treat others with respect, and when the opportunity presents itself engage human-to-human.

All those efforts can advance our new mission. We can create a society that's more equal, cooperative and peaceful than the one we have now — a society in which:
- individuals commit to self-development and support others in that effort;

- families raise healthy children;
- human- and social-service professionals nurture self- and community-empowerment;
- elected officials enact compassionate legislation;
- concerned individuals devote at least a few hours a month to political action.

This compassionate society would oppose racism, sexism, extreme economic inequality, political corruption, Big Money ruling politics, the prison-industrial complex, militarism, materialism, selfishness, and all other forms of injustice, oppression and dehumanization.

In assessing national well-being, the traditional focus is on the gross domestic product (GDP), which measures material production. But the GDP does not consider non-material factors. The United Nations' World Happiness Report offers an alternative measure. In 2017 the United States ranked 14th overall in national happiness — but only because it ranked 9th in GDP per person. On every other measure, the U.S. was lower that 14th. And its overall score had declined since the previous report.[107]

America can do better than that. We can honor our highest ideals and set aside structures and habits that conflict with those ideals. Rather than being driven by fear, we can create a society that is grounded in respect and dignity for all.

5: Evolutionary Revolution

How can we activists improve how we operate?
How can we overcome divisions, such as those shaped
by race, class, and gender? What strategies will help us succeed?

Majorities of the American people agree on many proposed changes in national policy that would move us toward a more compassionate society.[108] Massive, united, grassroots movements that push for those changes could help establish those policies. To be successful in that effort, compassionate Americans need to reach out beyond their comfort zone, help turn majorities into super-majorities, and inspire passive supporters to become active supporters.

To build that power, we activists need to improve how we treat each other, how we communicate with those who disagree, how we recruit supporters, and how we decide on a course of action. Too often, we neglect self-examination, are judgmental toward others and ourselves, and fail to operate democratically. Those habits undermine our effectiveness.

If we listen to our conscience and love all humanity, we can help each other become better, more engaged, more moral human beings. We can change what we can and accept what we cannot change or escape, while waiting for another day when new circumstances create opportunities for more change, recognizing we'll never change certain aspects of reality. Admitting mistakes and apologizing for them can help us set aside divisive habits such as arrogance, egotism, dogmatism, individualism, bias, and the lust for power over others.

If we're determined and support one another, we can help transform America. If other countries do the same, we can create a more peaceful world and save the planet as a place fit for human life.

To transform this nation into a compassionate community, we Americans will have to constantly measure ourselves by the standards set by Charter for Compassion: Do our actions avoid both selfishness and self-sacrifice? Do they serve me and my neighbor? Do they serve my nation and all humanity? Does my company serve the public interest as well as earn a profit? Is my activist organization too concerned with building its own power, rather than forming coalitions to build people power? Am I too concerned with myself, my family, and my community? Am I giving to receive, or are my gifts authentic? Am I being self-indulgent, or am I taking care of myself to avoid burnout?

Answering those questions requires difficult, honest self-examination and the willingness to see reality from multiple perspectives. Most of all it requires humility: the ability to empathize with and understand others, to be righteous without being self-righteous, to make judgments without being judgmental, to live the way you want others to live while accepting that they need to do the same.

I hardly know why I do what I do, much why others do what they do. But one thing is clear: the real reasons for our actions are often deep, gut-level reactions and intuitions, and our intellectual explanations are rationalizations. When that's the case, arguments about ideas can be fruitless. Instead, before we can have a real conversation, we need to first find common ground, acknowledge shared underlying values, and establish mutual respect and trust.

In politics, analyzing the pros and cons of policy alternatives can be an endless merry-go-round. As partisanship has intensified, each tribe seeks to crush the other. They mobilize their troops by launching personal attacks and provoking fear, aided and abetted by the mainstream media that profit from "crossfire" debates and partisan conflict. They don't really try to understand their opponents or why they find certain arguments persuasive. Instead they set up straw men to attack and manipulate people by provoking fear.

But neuroscientists are confirming that humans react with less fear when they're reminded that they're loved or could be loved.[109] Performers and athletes learn to transcend fear by accepting it. During natural disasters and other emergencies people often display remarkable daring. Soldiers in battle report that solidarity with and compassion for their comrades motivate them to persist. Courage, caring and calm are contagious. We need not be victims of fear. The same applies to anger, which doesn't necessarily lead to hate. Being compassionate with one another helps us manage both fear and anger.

Many if not most Democrats don't acknowledge that Trump supporters are only one-third of the population with understandable reasons for resentment and anger. The System's top-level administrators have long disrespected them and disregarded their legitimate needs. Key examples are towns and cities that witness their young people move away in droves as their economies dry up. The Establishment, despite its rhetoric, seems not to care.

Democrats shouldn't even condemn as less than human those Trump supporters who are die-hard racists. Most people are prejudiced to some degree. That prejudice is easily inflamed. And many full-blown racists are in many respects decent human beings who've been duped and manipulated by those who divide and conquer.

In a similar vein, many if not most Republicans fail to acknowledge that black and brown people are a relatively powerless minority who are resentful and angry for understandable reasons. Police officers often disrespect people of color, abuse them, and lock them up more frequently than they do whites for the same crime. And some officers kill them for no good reason. Moreover, it's been proven that many Americans unfairly discriminate against people of color and don't actively support efforts to correct that injustice. Instead, they scapegoat people of color and overlook the fact that we could all do much better if the top one percent didn't take twenty percent of the nation's annual income and one-third of the nation's wealth.

+++++

We'll likely never build community with large numbers of rabid racists who have nothing but contempt for people of color. But we can build bridges with some. One powerful example is the black man at a demonstration who approached a neo-Nazi whose shirt was covered with swastikas, calmly asked him for a hug, and then asked, "Why do you hate me?" His response was "I don't know." The encounter may have opened a door.

Connecting with those whose racism is less rabid is more likely. A similar dilemma applies to urban elites who have nothing but contempt for rural "riff raff." We need to dissolve their prejudice as well.

If we want to build powerful grassroots movements, we need as much support as we can get. We need to keep the door open to everyone, including rural racists and arrogant cosmopolitans. Even if our top priority is solidifying community with those who are easiest to recruit, some effort can be devoted to reaching beyond the choir. We can learn from others and we usually don't know beforehand when an alliance might form.

If we more fully love ourselves and our opponents, we'll more likely find common ground and reconciliation. Even when others do horrible things, we can hate the sin but not the sinner. Without excusing misdeeds or demonizing, we can look for ways to unite and fight for universal policies that benefit all working people, white, black, and brown, rural and urban, from all income levels (as well as policies that target specific disinherited populations). Those victories will nourish compassion, erode the frustrations that engender hate, and build up our opponents' positive qualities.

At the same time, we can directly engage those who fear that black and brown people will take their jobs, discuss their fears, and address how their needs can be fulfilled without oppressing others. "When you win, I must lose" is a myth. We can both win. In fact, win-win is the only way to really win.

+++++

We can help one another become more fully human by cultivating proactive, compassionate, nonviolent communities whose members refuse to scapegoat. "You hurt my feelings" is one example of scapegoating. Hurt feelings don't result from a single cause. In those situations, many factors are at play, including our own responsibility for feeling hurt. I filter others' words and actions with my thinking. How I interpret that behavior is key, as is the mood I'm in. Sometimes a statement or action may get under my skin. At other times, it's like water off a duck's back and I say to myself, "That's his problem."

"Sticks and stones may break my bones, but words will never break me" is an old African-American folk adage that holds wisdom. It was first recorded in print in 1862 in a publication of the African Methodist Episcopal Church.[110] Drawing on that tradition, the great African-American theologian, Howard Thurman, a mentor to Dr. Martin Luther King, Jr. wrote:

> ...Anyone who permits another to determine the quality of his inner life gives into the hands of the other the key to his destiny. If a man knows precisely what he can do to you or what epithet he can hurl against you in order to make you lose your temper, your equilibrium, then he can always keep you under subjection.[111]

The Dalai Lama said:

You have to think: Why did this happen? This person is not your enemy from birth.... You see that this person's actions are due to their own destructive emotions. You can develop a sense of concern, compassion, even feel sorry for their pain and suffering.[112]

Rather than say, "You hurt me," it's more constructive to say, "When you said X, I felt Y." With that language, the focus is on the action, not the person. "You hurt me" can be seen as a *personal* attack, an ad hominem challenge to the other at her core. That phrase can make the exchange more heated and lead to a reciprocal, escalating blame game in which each party accuses the other. In the end, such altercations often degenerate into name-calling.

One result of those blame games is personal defensiveness. People become less likely to speak honestly, because they're afraid they will "cause harm" or be accused of causing harm. That fear gives power to people who are prone to level the charge "You hurt me." Accusers can manipulate others by sending them on guilt trips. And when "defendants" plead not guilty, "prosecutors" often punish, shun, or excommunicate them. As a result, former allies are frequently splintered off. In many cases, potential allies, faced with the threat of such harsh judgments, choose to preemptively withdraw from political engagement and operate in a safer, apolitical environment — causing still more splintering.

Society should discourage cruel words and hate speech that lead to hurt feelings and hold people accountable for the consequences of their actions, especially when they violate the law. But when cruel words contribute to hurt feelings, we shouldn't dehumanize those who use those words. Experience shows that when we do, they tend to double-down on their toxic attacks. Name-calling becomes a self-fulfilling prophecy. Rather than publicly "call out" associates with harsh judgments, we can instead, with compassionate criticisms, "call in" by inviting others to avoid similar mistakes in the future and join with us to move forward.

A kind response to cruel words can be placed within the framework of transforming the System and pointing out that the real problem is the System. That approach avoids placing excessive blame on individuals, which reinforces individualism. It makes no sense to demonize any individual or look for a Savior. We can humbly refrain from exaggerating our own responsibility and lift a burden from our shoulders by not trying to be a Savior ourselves. If we Americans cultivate such changes in our attitudes and values, we'll be better able to build a unified grassroots movement strong enough to make major changes in our culture and institutions.

To build massive unity, we need to overcome those tendencies. By recovering our deep human capacity for compassion, we can expose the System's hypocrisy, advance collaboration, make clear that selfish gain at the expense of others is immoral, and insist that society live up to its highest ideals. We can use the System's own ideals to transform the System into a force that empowers everyone to live the life they want to live.

+++++

We can grow small bands of trusted allies who create social greenhouses that serve as models for the society we seek. Such groups can help their members learn to respect one another as individuals of equal worth, liberate their inner hunter-gatherer, stop being mean to each other, and realize their spiritual potential. Activist organizations, *with intention*, can help their members support one another in their open-ended, self-defined personal growth, rather than leaving it to natural human support (which happens less frequently these days).

Even if you don't call yourself "religious" or "spiritual," chances are you appreciate many nonmaterial realities —

such as love, beauty, and the human mind. If you do, I consider you spiritual. Those nonmaterial realities prompt people to use terms like spirit, soul, God, life force, Ground of Being, and Higher Power. Flesh is always enspirited and spirit is always enfleshed. We are whole. Nonmaterial and material realities are equally important.

The most important truths can't be captured by words. They're preverbal. That's why we need poets, painters, musicians and other artists to help get in touch with those realities that leave us speechless, awestruck, overwhelmed. When we're lucky, we tap our intuition, learn from our dreams, and otherwise allow our unconscious to express itself, like when writers feel they're a conduit for a voice from beyond. Maybe that's why Jesus said, "Become like little children." [113]

Systemic reform involves spiritual growth as well as material changes. You can't touch a system. Systems consist of the relationships between the individual elements that compose the System. Such relationships are nonmaterial. They're the space between the elements of the system. These realities are not concrete. They have no boundaries and can't be measured. The System is not a machine ruled by cause-and-effect.

Those issues relate to politics. Activists tend to place too much emphasis on the written word, public policies, actions in the material world, and, usually, measurable results. Concrete victories are important, but no one victory is worth using any means to achieve it.

Neither is any one victory worth intentional self-sacrifice. At times we may risk our life or lose it. And others may believe we've sacrificed the good life, when in fact we've gained profound satisfaction in hard, meaningful work. Nevertheless, if activists take care of themselves for the long haul, we can better become the change we seek, love ourselves as we love others, avoid burnout, and improve our ability to be effective.

The process is as important as the product. The spiritual is as important as the material. In the silence of our solitude and with trusted allies, we can acknowledge our mistakes and resolve not to repeat them. And day-by-day, in our neighborhoods, on the streets of our towns, in elevators, and wherever we go, we can make eye contact, smile, nod, and in some way, say, "Hello in there, fellow human being." Bit by bit, we can humanize the world.

Ideally, reforms we enact will establish new structures that establish lasting improvements and shift the balance of power. But we shouldn't forget that, sometimes, band-aids are also useful to alleviate suffering. In any case, we can make it clear to everyone that no one victory is final. We'll never achieve Utopia. With that understanding, we can avoid allowing minor reforms to reinforce the System by giving the impression that those reforms are sufficient.

Absent a broader, long-term context, single-issue projects reinforce individualism and buttress the notion that only separate organizations are feasible. Activists need not always talk about their overarching long-term mission. Social service agencies can help individuals cope. Innovators can build new models like farmers' markets. Neighborhood associations can fight for STOP signs. Families can focus on their children. At the same time, those efforts can operate within the context of a long-term, transformative mission.

By being explicit about an underlying commitment to systemic reform, such efforts can increase awareness, plant seeds, and nudge people toward helping to build a transformative movement that includes concrete political action to improve national policies. Waiting rooms can have transformative literature on the coffee tables and transformative art on the walls. Organizational brochures can mention the underlying mission. Social-service agencies can distribute literature discussing political actions. Psychotherapists can nurture deeper purposes and insights.

Without a shared, broader commitment to a long-term mission, change efforts are more likely to stay fragmented. Individuals and organizations are more likely to stay excessively concerned with their own self-interest. With a compelling vision and contagious joy, however, we can attract others to join us, help one another sharpen our thinking, become better human beings, and act to improve public policies, especially national policies that are the source of so many of our local problems, such as homelessness.

Eventually we can end up with a transformed society, one that is fundamentally and comprehensively new. But we can't force it or predict it. As the *Bhagavad Gita* says, "The work is yours, but not the fruits thereof."[114] All we can do is improve the world, person by person, community by community, institution by institution, all at the same time, step by step, day by day, minute by minute — and see how it goes

As we build momentum with progress, new possibilities may enable majority support to form behind proposals previously considered unrealistic and we may experience never-ending evolutionary revolution.

6: Leadership

What forms of leadership are most effective?
Is leadership always defined by the ability to mobilize others?
Must leaders always be in charge? How should victims
of oppression have more voice in how to deal with it?

Traditional leaders mobilize followers to do what the leader wants. Collaborative leaders help groups agree on the problem they want to confront and facilitate decision-making to solve the problem.

When egalitarian hunter-gatherers moved into city-states, they established militaries to protect themselves and their food. Those militaristic societies needed top-down power to implement decisions quickly. Similar patterns have permeated ever since.

When industrial businesses developed, they established military-style bureaucracies to control their workers. Then, in the late 19th century, large businesses began to control the chaos of the free market by creating monopolies and oligopolies.[115] When governments established social-welfare programs to protect their citizens from the ravages of the free market, they too relied on military-style bureaucracies and top-down leadership.[116]

Descriptions of traditional leadership have included:

- *To lead is to direct the operations, activity, or performance of; to have charge of.[117]*
- *A leader is one who knows the way, goes the way, and shows the way.[118]*
- *I'll tell you what leadership is. It's persuasion, and conciliation, and education, and patience.[119]*
- *The leader has the vision and the rest is a sales problem.[120]*
- *Leaders still need to set the vision and ensure everybody buys in.[121]*

- *Leadership on the world stage ... allows you to define and set the rules of the game more than any other player, and to do so in a way that advances your interests and shapes the world to reflect your values.[122]*
- *It is a prime responsibility of those leading change to always be clear about what's on or off the table for discussion.[123]*
- *The leader is one who mobilizes others toward a goal shared by leaders and followers.[124]*
- *Leadership molds individuals into a team.[125]*

Critics of relying too heavily on traditional leadership have said:

- *Most leaders die with their mouths open.[126]*
- *Quit telling/Start asking: The best bosses accept that they don't have all the answers. They use a lot of open-ended questions that start with: How, Where, Why, When. When I meet a leader who thinks (s)he knows more than the collective team, I know there is a big problem. Either that person is full of himself or the entire team needs to be replaced. Not surprisingly, it's usually the former.[127]*
- *That notion of leadership is bankrupt. It only works for technical problems where there's a right answer and an expert knows what it is.*

The *Leader to Leader* journal publishes innovative work on leadership by numerous insightful writers, including Peter Senge, Daniel Goleman, Bill George, and John Carver. A particularly compelling piece was "The Art of Chaordic Leadership"[128] by Dee Hock. In that essay, Hock combined the words chaos and order to coin the term "chaordic" and concluded:

In the deepest sense, distinction between leaders and followers is meaningless. In every moment of life, we are simultaneously leading and following.... We were all born leaders; that is, until we were sent to school and taught to be managed and to manage. People are not "things" to be manipulated, labeled, boxed, bought, and sold.... We are entire human beings.... We must examine the concept of superior and subordinate with increasing skepticism.... It is true leadership — leadership by everyone — chaordic leadership, in, up, around, and down that this world so badly needs, and industrial age, dominator management that it so sadly gets.[129]

In *Boards That Make a Difference: A New Design for Leadership in Nonprofit and Public Organizations,* John Carver suggests shared leadership, or partnership, between boards and staff. With a separation of co-equal powers between board and staff, boards can establish written goals to guide staff, delegate to staff the responsibility to implement those policies, and periodically evaluate staff.

Board members who agree on their primary mission come together as equals. Everyone can exercise leadership. At any one time, anyone might suggest a step that makes sense to the others and moves the group forward. The chair facilitates this decision-making, without necessarily guiding it. And the board-as-a-whole leads the organization.[130]

In recent decades, the corporate world has increasingly adopted various self-management methods. Holacracy, the best-known form of this innovation, defines roles around the work, not individuals, and relies on teams, with individuals typically filling several roles.[131] Authority to make key decisions is delegated to those teams, which self-organize. Everyone is bound by the same rules, including the chief executive officer. Rules are visible to all. According to a lengthy evaluation in the *Harvard Business Review,* the result is often

an organization that is responsive to the requirements of the work rather than to the directives of any powerful individual.... For such agency to thrive, both managers and subordinates must unlearn old behaviors.... Ultimately, and somewhat ironically, the next generation of self-managing teams is demanding a new generation of leaders – senior individuals with the vision to see where it is best to set aside hierarchy for another way of operating, but also with the courage to defend hierarchy where it serves the institution's fundamental goals.[132]

Those lessons from the corporate world are relevant to grassroots political organizing. Grassroots organizing needs carefully structured democratic control. In the classic 1971 essay, "The Tyranny of Structurelessness," Jo Freeman argued there's no such thing as a structureless group.[133] Power is hidden when it's denied. A division of labor and clear lines of responsibility, with groups electing their leaders, is necessary for democratic accountability.

Numerous labor and activist organizations have established bottom-up methods for membership control. Worker-owned cooperatives have demonstrated that horizontal structures can work (and help prevent businesses relocating to other countries). The Next System Project, a project of the Democracy Collaborative, is doing important work as "a research and development lab for political-economic alternatives."[134] Since 2010, thirty-three states have authorized "benefit corporations" that commit to serving their workers and the public interest as well as earning a profit, which nurtures greater democratic accountability.[135]

Kingian nonviolence seeks reconciliation. Nonviolent direct action aims to build enough pressure to bring opponents to the negotiating table in search of compromise. The intent is not to defeat "enemies." There's no assumption that the activist group holds enough wisdom to force its opponents to do everything it wants. No individual or collective has the final, complete answer.

Collaboration is key. A collaborative process helps to gain "buy-in" from members, who are more likely to actively support decisions because they've had a real voice in making them. And participatory democracy helps to dissolve the deep-seated tendency to automatically submit to authority.

Professional political organizers often convene workshops on how to talk **to** potential supporters to mobilize them. And they conduct training sessions on how to conduct initial interviews to surface new members' interests. But organizers rarely convene workshops on how to really talk **with** members, day by day. Real dialogue involves listening.

Democracy accepts "the wisdom of crowds." When a group is careful and deliberate, it can generally make wiser decisions than any one person can. "Two heads are better than one," and three are better yet. Humans often think best when they think together. There's no guarantee, of course, but the odds are improved, especially when the group is diverse rather than homogenous.

Diversity provides a wide array of information and perspectives, which can be incorporated into decision-making. The greater the diversity, the more likely the resulting decisions will be wise. Since all people are affected by every issue, everyone is entitled to a voice in helping society overcome its many divisions.

When a group is addressing an issue that focuses on a particular group, such as domestic abuse that victimizes women or police brutality against black and brown people, it makes sense to have representatives from those populations more heavily represented in the decision-making about how to address the problem. They're likely to better understand the issue, and others would be wise to pay special attention to their recommendations. But to expect others to always follow the recommendations of victim-group representatives would reinforce the System's pattern of nurturing domination and submission.

Moreover, everyone has multiple identities. We're positioned differently on multiple "ladders of success," and those ladders intersect one another. Individuals may hold a different degree of power on each ladder. To say that you should defer to others who are more disadvantaged on one ladder may miss the fact that you are more disadvantaged on another ladder.

One example of this complication, which is often overlooked, relates to whether someone has a college degree. The one-third of Americans who are college-educated gain arbitrary advantages due to their schooling. They often discriminate against those who have no degree. And those without degrees are often resentful toward those with degrees. That creates a major barrier to social unity. But many professional, college-educated community organizers don't deal with that issue or even acknowledge it. Their own bias blinds them to an important problem.

Leader-full democratic collaboration is not easy. But it can cultivate one key form of leadership: the power of example. And it's essential if we are going to transform the System.

7: A Mutual Support Method

What easy-to-learn method could be widely used to provide mutual support for self-development and political activism?

Small mutual support teams that embrace shared values and principles can nurture self-development. In *Join the Club: How Peer Pressure Can Transform the World*, Tina Rosenberg reports that "from the affluent suburbs of Chicago to the impoverished shanties of rural India" mutual support teams have helped smokers stop smoking, teens fight AIDS, worshippers deepen their faith, activists overthrow dictators, addicts overcome addictions, and students learn calculus.[136]

Such teams could also help compassion-minded individuals set aside counter-productive tendencies and become more effective — and inspire politically inactive people to become more active. Those teams could serve as social greenhouses where we could develop our ability to relate as equals, create models, and strengthen our ability to help transform the world.

Small circles of trusted allies could help one another undo society's negative conditioning. We could learn to become more compassionate, realize our potential more fully, avoid hate-filled scapegoating, stop being so mean to one another, and diminish discrimination. As we solidify those habits, we could expand them into the larger society, relying heavily on the power of example.

To confess is at the heart of every religion. It's the path to redemption, being reborn, becoming a new person — and essential to help organizations recognize mistakes and grow. As individuals, we can of course do a lot on our own — privately within our own minds — to promote self-development. But we can also support one another in that effort. Verbalizing to others helps us better understand our thoughts and feelings. And listening to others is often a learning experience. We can accomplish more, and achieve deeper growth, by engaging in mutual support than we can by acting alone.

Many historical examples illustrate the power of small, supportive groups. The disciples who followed Jesus were a group of twelve, and Christian house churches based on the "priesthood of all believers" have been potent for centuries. Many political organizations have used affinity groups, precinct-based teams, cells, neighborhood organizations, and other constellations. Book clubs, poker games, bowling leagues, gangs, various "posses," and other such groups all provide informal support.

The Bushmen in southern Africa, who lived in small bands, had a ritual, "insulting the meat," that helped them maintain their egalitarian society. When a hunter returned with a large kill, he'd be greeted with light-hearted, inaccurate insults about the quality of the kill or the level of his skill. It was a way to discourage the hunter from thinking too highly of himself. Such methods to nurture humility benefited everyone.[137]

Alcoholics Anonymous and other twelve-step programs have demonstrated the effectiveness of self-governing, self-perpetuating communities based on: 1) concise core principles, and; 2) a consistent, easy-to-learn format that facilitates self-improvement without extensive training. In such programs, the willingness to openly, honestly admit mistakes is key to the healing process.

The True North Groups initiated in the corporate world by Bill George developed a more open-ended approach. Rather than focus on a particular issue, such as substance abuse or Bible study, or training people on particular skills, those groups nurture deeper intimacy by means of radical openness. Each participant can discuss anything.[138]

With that kind of open-ended approach, political activists committed to compassionate, systemic transformation could gather with other activists to support one another in their self-improvement. Activists, after all, are often as addicted to activism as twelve-step members are addicted to mind-altering substances. We could encourage the development of communities whose members **set aside time** to support one another in an **open-ended** manner with: 1) their personal efforts to become better human beings, and; 2) their political efforts to help improve national public policy.

To the best of my knowledge, no such community exists. Some excellent organizations nurture both personal and political transformation. Examples include the Church for the Fellowship of All Peoples, Glide Memorial Church, #LoveArmy, Mujeres Unidas y Activas, National Domestic Workers Alliance, Network of Spiritual Progressives, and Thrive East Bay. However, it seems there's no organization that uses an easy-to-learn method to help its members **set aside time** to provide **open-ended** mutual support for self-improvement and political action. Once such a method is established, a wide range of other groups could use it — and join a growing, larger community.

To maximize its effectiveness, any such project would need to avoid authoritarianism of the kind reflected in Chairman Mao's reeducation program in China in the 1960s and in social rehab programs like Synanon in the Bay Area in the 1970s, which were based on vicious, judgmental "criticism-self-criticism." One way to prevent authoritarianism is to borrow from the Harm Reduction model, which, instead of demanding total abstinence, asks individuals to define their own substance abuse goals.[139] Another way to minimize authoritarianism is to have individuals simply report on their self-development efforts, with no "cross-talk" from others. Twelve-step programs take that approach.

In those ways, mutual support team members could help one another gradually loosen the System's top-down conditioning and cultivate positive new habits to carry into the larger society. Bit by bit, they could liberate their inner hunter-gatherer, increase their self-knowledge, learn to relate as equals, and become more cooperative, peaceful, and playful. Undoing old habits often requires intentional effort, but with dedication and the willingness to be vulnerable, all of us who seek a more compassionate society can move down that path.

Personal transformation is rarely a matter of sudden, total, irreversible conversion. Rather, it's a gradual, ongoing process. We often fall back into old ways of operating. Two steps forward, one step back. Perfection, permanent salvation, and total enlightenment are not possible. We can only do our best, knowing we're good enough and can be better. Pragmatic idealism is the wisest path.

Being open, honest, and vulnerable with close friends can be difficult. It's easy to withdraw or focus on work, play, or superficial interactions. That reluctance may be especially true with political activists who are driven to reduce suffering and injustice. It seems to them there's not a minute to waste and self-examination is self-indulgent navel gazing. But in the long run self-criticism and mutual support can nurture self-improvement and enhance effectiveness.

Given that perspective, what easy-to-learn method could be widely used to provide mutual support for self-development and political activism? The method proposed here is to grow a network of small, mutual support teams whose members:

- endorse the same mission statement, such as the one proposed in this draft declaration;
- commit themselves to become more compassionate individuals and more effective activists;
- report to one another about their personal and political change efforts at least once a month;
- meet occasionally with members from other teams in the network;
- nurture a spirit of community within and between teams.

The monthly reports, which would be confidential, could begin with a minute or two of silence to enable members to reflect, meditate, or pray. Members would then respond to this question: "What are you feeling and thinking about your personal and political change efforts?"

It would be clear that each member defines their own goals. There would be no pressure to correct any behavior. And there might be no "cross-talk" or other interaction during those reports.

Team members would, of course, support one another informally in many other ways. Feedback and advice could be offered informally later, ideally with consent. Additional meetings could be scheduled to go into issues more deeply. But all that would be optional. The only requirement would be the brief monthly report.

Reporting regularly can help hold us accountable for our commitments. Knowing we'd be asked to report, we'd be more conscious of our commitments during the month and more likely act on them. Since each member might report for only sixty seconds once a month, why not do it?

Regardless of their political or religious perspective, different kinds of groups could join such a network. Those groups include:

- a committee within an activist organization;
- a book club;
- a religious organization's social action committee or Bible study group;
- a work group at a socially responsible business;
- a group whose members belong to various activist organizations or do their activism as unaffiliated individuals.

Many groups could also share a meal and socialize informally as a way for members to get to know one another more fully. Time permitting, larger meetings could ask members to report briefly on their personal growth efforts as well as their political actions during introductions. Activist organizations could adopt official policies to encourage their members to support one another with their self-development. Residents of other countries could join the network, endorse its mission statement, and form mutual support teams to advance it. Individuals who do not participate themselves might see the value for others and tell them about it.

If you have thoughts about other methods for how compassion-minded individuals and organizations might nurture mutual support, self-development, and political action — or know of others who do — please share those ideas and information. And if you want to experiment with other methods, please do so and let us know what happens.

The basic goal is simple: an easy-to-learn method that people could use to support one another in their personal and political change efforts — a method that could spread widely and quickly as did the twelve-step method.

The method presented here seems to hold great potential for achieving that goal and growing a large community of people who endorse the same mission and use the same method for pursuing that mission. My life experience with many forms of mutual support and my experiments with and conversations about this method give me confidence in its potential to help transform the System — so everyone can be all they can be.

How that network of mutual support teams, or the other projects previously mentioned, might develop is another question, to be addressed next in the Conclusion.

Conclusion

This draft declaration is based on the belief that humanity needs to build massive, grassroots movements dedicated to transforming our world into a compassionate community in which each nation is dedicated to the common good of all humanity, its own people, the environment, and life itself. With this approach, each nation can focus on its own needs in a way that is harmonious with the needs of other nations and the planet. We can restore the balance between trust and fear.

Addressing the root causes of needless suffering is made easier if we concentrate on winnable demands that already have majority support and move in the direction of that long-term goal. Achieving such goals can contribute to evolutionary revolution.

Building that movement will require unlearning many aspects of our social conditioning. We can do that more fully if we discuss our efforts with a small group of like-minded individuals who share the same commitment to global, systemic transformation.

To move in that direction, identifying strongly as a member of the human family is an urgent necessity. No task is more important. Adopting a world-centric perspective that affirms the inherent worth of all humans is critical. Doing so will help us treat each other with respect.

We aren't merely an individual. We hold many other identities, such as a member of a family, race, gender, class, or nation. We may also identify with a religion, community organization, political party, or other voluntary association. We need not drop those identities. But they aren't separate. They're woven into one fabric. At our core we are essentially a human being.

If membership in a tribe becomes overwhelming, we forget our shared humanity. Self-interest and tribal interest merge, and tribal membership stands over against another tribe. Trying to better understand the opponent as a fellow human is beside the point: defeating "the enemy." Revenge is key. Scapegoating is routine. Any way to win is justified. The only solution is to impose one's will. One's own issue becomes the only one that matters. Tribal leaders can do anything; their tribe follows regardless.

Nonviolent demonstrations that create brief inconvenience can be effective, especially if they focus on winnable demands. Outside forces can take stronger stands than do inside decision-makers. Different people play different roles. Heat is often needed to place an issue on the table. There is a difference between right and wrong. Militant demands for justice are needed.

But both forces, inside and outside, need to understand each other's motives without trying to totally discredit the other. We can be righteous without being-self-righteous. We can remember that no one individual or group holds all the answers. We can be willing to discuss, negotiate, and compromise, while remaining open to reconciliation.

"Any means necessary" is immoral and does not work. There are limits to what methods are justified. Moreover, crossing that ethical line can be counter-productive. Most people desire order for understandable reasons. We need to respect the desire to avoid chaos. Hurting others is no way to gain support.

And we need to avoid demonizing our opponents. We can criticize their actions without denying their humanity, condemning them as worthless. To dehumanize is no way to fight dehumanization.

We must overcome our selfish, competitive individualism and rebuild the compassionate cooperation that enabled humans to evolve beyond our ape ancestors. We must continue to domesticate ourselves and nurture trust and cooperation — characteristics that were bred into our DNA by 200,000 years of human evolution as hunter-gatherers suppressed their "alpha male" tendencies to bully and dominate.

Every religion has included a form of the Golden Rule. Our Declaration of Independence affirmed that everyone is created equal. The United Nations adopted the Universal Declaration of Human Rights.[140] When he landed on the moon, Neil Armstrong declared, "That's one small step for a man, one giant leap for *mankind*."[141] Disaster relief efforts reflect enormous compassion for strangers in distant lands.

One group competing against another is one way to induce a sense of community that transcends the ego. But it is not the only way. Immersion in nature and religious experiences with music, dancing, and worship, for example, do not involve competition. As we humans continue to evolve, we can cultivate a stronger commitment to those universal moral rules that guide us to treat all humans with compassion.[142] The universal threat posed by climate change could reinforce that kind of co-evolution between culture and biology. The need to unite and affirm our common humanity becomes clearer daily.

We must always ask: Do I love others as I love myself? Do I love my "enemies"? Am I avoiding both selfishness and self-sacrifice? Am I treating others as I want to be treated? Can my nation, my community, and I hold firmly to our beliefs without demanding that your nation, your community, and you affirm the same beliefs? If I am a white Christian, must I demand that the United States be a white Christian nation? To defend my nation, must I insist that America dominate the world? Or is peaceful cooperation between countries possible? Can all humans seek to transform their nation into a compassionate community? Can all my identities thrive at the same time? Can it be both/and? Can win-win work? Can I benefit when you benefit? Or is life zero-sum? If you win, must I lose?

The Internet makes compassionate global community more possible than ever. To move in that direction, we Americans must set a positive example. America originally committed herself to "promote the *general* welfare." "Barn raising" symbolized the American spirit. Responses to natural catastrophes bring out our higher angels.

But most of us tell our children to "get ahead" of the competition, climb social ladders, look down on those below, and "you can be whatever they want to be." We preach "what's in it for me?" and "it's all about me (and my family)." Many men still declare "Father knows best," "Someone must always be in charge," and "I am the King around here, so don't forget it!" White politicians tell poor whites, "You got more than the blacks, you're better than them."[143] People avoid their own responsibility, ignore the power of the System, and scapegoat enemies with hate-filled rhetoric — rather than mobilize a broad-based supermajority behind a positive vision to improve living conditions. And as America spreads its selfish individualism throughout the world, it inflames tribal divisions elsewhere.

All that conditioning makes it difficult for Americans to relate to one another as individuals with equal rights and equal essential value. We spend most of our time dominating or submitting, which becomes a habit. When the situation calls for forming equal partnerships, it's often not easy, even when everyone wants it. That reality calls us to commit to self-improvement: to become better human beings.

But if we try to dictate specific answers, we undermine liberty and self-determination and encourage people to escape personal responsibility by automatically submitting to power, whether legitimate or not. How to implement those communal principles needs to be a personal decision. Individuals are responsible for their own answer. We can live the way we want others to live while accepting their right to do the same. We can ask others, "How do you want to be a better person?" without pressing them to live the way we want them to live. We can share our ideas while leaving it to others to answer that question for themselves.

That's the approach this draft declaration has tried to take. It suggests answers to key questions, not as the final word but as food for thought, trusting that by thinking together we can develop better answers.

The assumption here is that infants and toddlers reveal human nature. They are naturally curious, caring, joyous, awestruck. The pursuit of truth, justice, and beauty strikes at the heart of what it means to be human. We are innately prone to be egalitarian, spiritual, compassionate, playful. The Golden Rule, which has basically been affirmed by every culture, captures a basic human truth: we want to treat others as we want to be treated. And we want to relieve suffering, which leads us to want to correct the causes of that suffering when we can.

That goal requires us to learn how to communicate respectfully when we disagree. We can embrace the best "conservative" values as well as the best "liberal" values. Contrary to "do your own thing" individualism, we can affirm loyalty to community and family. Contrary to "whatever's right" relativism, we can affirm that there is a difference between right and wrong. Contrary to those who say truth is relative, we can declare it's possible to know what's true. Contrary to those who always reject authority, we can accept the need for legitimate power. Contrary to "what's in it for me" selfishness, we can be concerned about all life. Contrary to those who look down on and feel superior to others, we can highlight what all humanity shares. Contrary to indifference to suffering, we can call for fairness to all humans and the protection of the environment. Contrary to those who crave chaos to help the System collapse, we can call for order rooted in justice. Contrary to those who aim to destroy or weaken the government, we can seek true democracy. That's the foundation on which this draft declaration is based.

This perspective is holistic. It addresses the whole person, including social ties, and the whole world. It aims to change the whole System. Liberating our inner hunter-gatherer, dissolving the System's conditioning, and building a powerful grassroots movement to transform the System will be no easy matter. The following steps can help.

Naming the System weakens it. We're immersed in a self-perpetuating global system with interwoven elements that reinforce one another. Those elements are our institutions, our culture, and ourselves as individuals. The System's driving force is the effort by individuals to gain more status, wealth, and power over others. By climbing social ladders, both ordinary people and elites build up their sense of self-worth and look down on those below, who they generally consider to be inferior. Relationships based on equality and mutual respect are rare. We learn to dominate or submit, which is the norm. Facing those realities makes it easier to change them, but that's only the first step.

Holistic communities engage the whole person and address weaknesses. To transform the System nation by nation, we must change ourselves. Small, supportive groups of individuals who share the same commitment can serve as social greenhouses that help their members become less self-centered, fearful, hateful, dishonest, competitive, judgmental, and hungry for power and status — and become more caring, trusting, joyous, honest, cooperative, accepting, and able to collaborate with others as individuals of equal worth. With individuals defining their own goals, we can become better human beings within healthy communities that cultivate authentic lives. For that growth to flourish, however, society-as-a-whole, the System, must change as well.

Seeing the whole system involves many-sided awareness. We can avoid getting stuck in ideology. We can be pragmatic idealists. We can make a difference *and* enjoy life. We can change the world *and* be the change. Families can care for their community *and* their children. Businesses can care for the public interest *and* their bottom line. Activist organizations can unite in coalitions *and* build their own organizations. Elected officials can use their office as an organizing tool *and* get re-elected. Nations can cooperate with other nations *and* take care of their own interests. It's both/and, not either/or. It's a matter of balance. If we all benefit, we all benefit.

Structure matters. A massive grassroots movement to promote democracy needs to be democratic, from the bottom up, without being bureaucratic. Small units can better give each member a voice, but even small units need to take care to avoid top-down domination by one or more members. Seeking consensus while relying on a super-majority when necessary can guard against both descending to the "lowest common denominator" and the tyranny of the minority by the majority. Local units can select representatives to regional units, who can select representatives to national bodies. Local units can be self-governing so long as they conform to national policies. A network of small support groups that embrace the same principles and use the same format to conduct meetings — like twelve-step groups do — would enable all participants to feel part of the same community, which would enrich the experience.

The most promising course to global transformation is evolutionary revolution: steady reforms that move in the direction of an agreed-on mission. Relying on the System to collapse so we can build on the ruins is an unreliable strategy that would accept widespread suffering. The future is unpredictable. The System may muddle through. Planning to destroy the system with a sudden forceful revolution is also unreliable, especially if it's violent. No violent revolution has worked; the victors have reproduced prior patterns of domination. Building on what we have and reforming it steadily with support from majorities of people holds more promise. No victory is final. By establishing a strong commitment to that never-ending struggle, we can avoid the risk that the System will co-opt reforms and undermine ongoing revolution.

Universal economic security is essential to systemic transformation. A compassionate society must assure that everyone has a decent opportunity to meet their basic needs. In the United States, a guaranteed living-wage job opportunity would be a key method to achieve that goal. It would give everyone a better chance to fulfill their potential and contribute to society. Those who want to climb a social ladder still could, but they wouldn't have to do so to avoid poverty. No child should have to grow up poor because their parents can't find a living-wage job. So long as some children have economic security and others do not, they're not equal. A plurality of Americans supports a federal jobs guarantee. A new federal bureaucracy would not be necessary. We could rely on federal revenue sharing to local governments to steadily increase funding for public-service, living-wage jobs until those jobs go begging due to lack of applicants. In developing countries, other methods might be needed to provide economic security in a way that reflects the prevailing standard of living in the local community. But there too, given the political will, steady progress to meet basic human needs can be achieved.

Efforts to transform the System need to be intentional and that intention needs to be written. Organizations adopt a mission statement and other written policies to focus their work. Married couples adopt wedding vows to guide their relationships. Systemic transformation projects also need to clarify their goals. Such affirmations help people hold one another accountable to their commitment.

+++++

One way to proceed would be for a diverse organizing committee to initiate one or more of the projects suggested in this draft declaration. Each project member could endorse the same pledge, such as:

- I will help transform my nation into a compassionate community dedicated to the common good of all humanity, our own people, the environment, and life itself.
- I will participate in a mutual support team whose members will, at least once a month, open their meetings with a minute or two of silence and then reply to this question: "What's happening with your personal and political change efforts?"
- My team will affiliate with [name of project] whose members also sign this pledge.

That approach would define "political" as "efforts to help change public policy." Those teams would presumably engage in other mutual support activities as well, but they would all use that same simple method at least once a month to open their meetings. That common embrace of the same mission and method would provide all team members with a shared experience that could nurture a sense of community. By doing so openly, they would encourage others to join the network. On occasion, regional, national, and global gatherings could enable members to inspire one another, publicize their efforts, and recruit more people to join the network.

+++++

Many people are engaged in personal or spiritual transformation, but most of them do not engage in political action with their colleagues. Separately, many people who engage in political action only support each other in their self-development efforts informally — they rarely collectively, openly support each other in those efforts.

The premise of this draft declaration is that many people in both groups — those who focus on the personal and those who focus on the political — could benefit by openly, consciously, and to some degree formally integrating their personal and political change efforts.

Some change agents are working on that kind of holistic, social transformation. But most of those efforts are led by professionals who work with full-time professional staff. One motive behind this draft declaration is to bring some of what those people have learned out into the public and encourage the development of a simple tool, within the framework of a shared core principle (as Alcoholics Anonymous did) that could spread widely and quickly. Doing so could help those activists increase their effectiveness. And it could encourage those who are inactive to become active.

Those needs seem urgent. This approach may be an idea whose time has come.

Or perhaps some other mutual support method would be more effective. If you're so inclined, please gather with three or more trusted friends, experiment with one or more ways to provide mutual support for your personal and political efforts and post a report about how it goes on TransformTheSystem.org. Or let us know of some such method already being employed.

The bottom line is: **develop an easy-to-learn method that individuals could use to support one another in their self-development and their political action** — a method that could scale up, spread quickly, and enable those who use it to identify as a member of the same community. Experimenting with such a model might prove to be like sticking a toe in the water. Those who do may jump in, pay the price James Baldwin talked about, become better human beings, and begin trusting one another more.

The paths to systemic transformation are many. The support method presented here is only one possibility. But it seems that an explicit, conscious commitment would help many people deepen their self-development and increase their political effectiveness.

While writing this draft declaration, I've experimented some with the method proposed here. The results were promising. If others experiment with other methods, or report on a similar ongoing project, we can compare notes and perhaps agree on the best way forward.

Consider meeting with a few friends to report on your personal and political change efforts. If you aren't sure how to proceed, share that uncertainty and brainstorm possibilities.

+++++

Please consider contributing to this effort in one of the following ways:

- purchase a few copies of *Transform the System: A Work in Progress* on Amazon and give them to people who may be interested;
- visit TransformTheSystem.org and post comments at the end of each chapter;
- spread the word about this project.

Soon I'll convene a workshop to evaluate this work-in-progress and agree on feedback. A report on comments posted on the website will be presented to workshop participants. Everyone who comments on the website and leaves their email address will be invited (email addresses will not be viewable or sold).

Other opportunities to collaborate may emerge as well. As I incorporate feedback and make new discoveries, I may update this declaration and post the latest version on the website.

For more info, see TransformTheSystem.org. Later, one possibility will be to find a publisher for an anthology with a revision to this declaration and essays written by others responding to the same question addressed here: What is "the system" and how should we change it?

This draft offers an answer to that question as food-for-thought, not the final word. Perhaps respondents will suggest major improvements to this approach. Perhaps others will start from scratch with a much different answer.

Time will tell, but the more we who are moving in the same direction support each other, the better our odds to help transform the System. Our chances are unknown. We can only do what we can do. Why not try?

Bibliography

Admati, Anat and Martin Hellwig, *The Bankers' New Clothes: What's Wrong with Banking and What to Do about It,* Princeton, Princeton University Press, 2013.

Alpert, Burt, *Inversions: A Study of Warped Consciousness,* Denver: Bradford Printing, 1972.

Baldwin, James, *Notes of a Native Son*, Boston: Beacon Press, 1955.

Baldwin, James, *Nobody Knows My Name: More Notes of a Native Son,* New York: Vintage International, 1961.

Baldwin, James, *Another Country,* New York: Vintage International, 1962.

Baldwin, James, *I Am Not Your Negro: A Major Motion Picture by Raoul Peck,* New York, Vintage International, 2017.

Bhikkhu, Amaro, *Small Boat, Great Mountain,* Redwood Valley: Abhayagiri Buddhist Monastery, 2003.

Bond, Becky and Zack Exley, *Rules for Revolutionaries: How Big Organizing Can Change Everything,* Whole River Junction: Chelsea Green Publishing, 2016.

Bookchin, Murray, *The Ecology of Freedom: The Emergence and Dissolution of Hierarchy*, Oakland, AK Press, 1982.

Bronner, Stephen Eric, *Camus: Portrait of a Moralist.* Chicago: University of Chicago, 1999.

Buber, Martin, *I and Thou.* New York: Scribner, 1958.

Butler, Christopher, *Postmodernism: A Very Short Introduction,* Oxford: Oxford University Press, 2002.

Cameron, Julia, *The Artist's Way: A Spiritual Path to Higher Creativity.* New York: Tarcher, Putnam, 1992.

Camus, Albert, *The Myth of Sisyphus and Other Essays.* New York: Random House, 1955.

Camus, Albert, *The Rebel: An Essay on Man in Revolt,* New York: Vintage International, 1956.

Camus, Albert, *Algerian Chronicles,* Cambridge: Belknap Press, 2013.

Crossan, John Dominic, *The Birth of Christianity: Discovering What Happened in the Years Immediately After the Execution of Jesus,* San Francisco: Harper, 1998.

Dinan, Stephen, *Sacred America, Sacred World: Fulfilling Our Mission in Service to All,* Charlottesville, Hampton Roads Publishing, 2016.

Emerson, Ralph Waldo, *The Portable Emerson,* New York: Viking Press, 1948.

Friere, Paolo, *Pedagogy of the Oppressed,* New York: Continuum, 1986.

Friedenberg, Edgar Z., *Coming of Age in America: Growth and Acquiescence,* New York: Vintage, 1965.

George, Bill and Doug Baker, *True North Groups: A Powerful Path to Personal and Leadership Development,* San Francisco: Berrett-Koehler, 2011.

Glassner, Barry, *The Culture of Fear: Why Americans Are Afraid of the Wrong Things: Crime, Drugs, Minorities, Teen Moms, Killer Kids, Mutant Microbes, Plane Crashes, Road Rage, & So Much More.* New York: Basic Books, 1999

Greider, William, *Secrets of the Temple: How the Federal Reserve Runs the Country,* New York: Simon & Schuster, 1987.

Haidt, Jonathan, *The Righteous Mind: Why Good People Are Divided by Politics and Religion,* New York: Random House, 2012.

Hartsough, David, *Waging Peace: Global Adventures of a Lifelong Activist,* Oakland, PM Press, 2014.

Heider, John, *The Tao of Leadership: Lao Tzu's* Tao Te Ching *Adapted for a New Age,* Atlanta: Humanics New Age, 1985.

Hoffman, Abbie, *Woodstock Nation: A Talk-Rock Album,* New York: Random House, 1969.

Horwitz, Claudia, *The Spiritual Activist: Practices to Transform Your Life, Your Work, and Your World,* New York: Penguin Compass, 2002.

Isenberg, Nancy, *White Trash: The 400-Year Untold History of Class in America,* New York: Viking Press, 2016.

Jacobs, Alan, *How to Think: A Survival Guide for a World at Odds,* New York: Penguin Random House, 2017.

Jaffe, Sarah, *Necessary Trouble: Americans in Revolt,* New York: Nation Books, 2016.

James, William, *The Varieties of Religious Experience: A Study in Human Nature,* Dover Publications, 1902.

Jones, Van, *Beyond the Messy Truth: How We Came Apart, How We Come Together,* New York: Ballantine Books, 2017.

Kahane, Adam, *Power and Love: A Theory and Practice of Social Change,* San Francisco: Berrett-Koehler, 2010.

Kahane, Adam, *Collaborating with the Enemy: How to Work with People You Don't Agree with or Like or Trust,* Oakland: Berrett-Koehler, 2017.

Kopkind, Andrew, ed., *Thoughts of the Young Radicals,* New Republic, 1968.

Laing, R.D., *The Politics of Experience,* New York: Ballantine, 1967.

Lakoff, George, *Moral Politics: How Liberals and Conservatives Think,* Chicago, University of Chicago Press, 1996.

Lama, Dalai and Desmond Tutu, *The Book of Joy: Lasting Happiness in a Changing World,* New York: Random House, 2016.

Leeds, Dorothy, *The 7 Powers of Questions,* New York: Perigee, 2000.

Loeb, Paul Rogat, *The Impossible Will Take a Little While, A Citizen's Guide to Hope in a Time of Fear,* New York: Basic Books, 2004.

Major, Reginald, *A Panther is a Black Cat,* New York: William Morrow and Company, 1971.

Marcuse, Herbert, *One-Dimensional Man: Studies in the Ideology of Advanced Industrial Society,* Boston: Beacon Press, 1964.

McLeod, Melvin, ed., *Mindful Politics: A Buddhist Guide to Making the World a Better Place,* Boston: Wisdom Publications, 2006.

Merton, Thomas, *Ishi Means Man,* Greensboro: Unicorn Press, 1968.

Merton, Thomas, *Love and Living,* San Diego: Harcourt Brace Jovanovich, 1979.

Millet, Kate, *Sexual Politics,* New York: Columbia University Press, 1969.

Mills, C. Wright, *The Power Elite,* New York: Oxford University Press, 1959.

Morgan. Robin, *Sisterhood is Powerful: An Anthology of Writings from the Women's Liberation Movement,* New York: Vintage, 1970.

Moyer, Bill, *Doing Democracy: The MAP Model for Organizing: The MAP Model for Organizing Social Movements,* Gabriola Island: New Society Publishers, 2001.

Nader, Ralph, *Breaking Through Power: It's Easier Than We Think,* San Francisco: City Lights, 2016.

Nagler, Michael N., *Is There No Other Way: The Search for a Nonviolent Future,* Berkeley: Berkeley Hills Books, 2001.

Needleman, Jacob, *Why Can't We Be Good?* New York: Tarcher/Penguin, 2007.

Nichols, Michael P., *The Lost Art of Listening: How Learning to Listen Can Improve Relationships,* New York: Guilford, Press, 1995.

Putnam, Robert D., *Bowling Alone: The Collapse and Revival of American Community,* New York: Simon & Schuster, 2000.

Reich, Charles A., *Opposing the System,* New York: Random House, 1995.

Rettig, Hillary, *The Lifelong Activist: How to Change the World Without Losing Your Way,* New York: Lantern Books, 2004.

Rosenberg, Tina, *Join the Club: How Peer Pressure Can Transform the World,* New York: W.W. Norton & Company, 2011.

Roszak, Theodore, *The Making of a Counter Culture,* Garden City: Doubleday, 1969.

Russell, Bertrand, *Bertrand Russell Speaks His Mind,* New York, Bard Books, 1960.

Ryan, William, *Blaming the Victim,* New York: Random House, 1971.

Salvatierra, Alexia and Peter Heltzel, *Faith Rooted Organizing: Mobilizing the Church in Service of the World,* Downers Grove, 2014.

Schutt, Randy, *Inciting Democracy, A Practical Proposal for Creating a Good Society,* Cleveland, Spring Forward Press, 2001.

Scott, James C., *Against the Grain: A Deep History of the Earliest States,* New Haven: Yale University Press, 2017.

Sennett, Richard and Jonathan Cobb, *The Hidden Injuries of Class,* New York: Random House, 1973.

Sennett, Richard, *Respect in a World of Inequality,* New York: W.W. Norton & Company, 2003.

Shaw, Randy, *The Activist Handbook: A Primer,* Berkeley: University of California Press, 1996.

Snyder, Gary, *Earth House Hold: Technical Notes & Queries To Fellow Dharma Revolutionaries,* York: New Directions, 1957.

Suzuki, Shunryu, *Zen Mind, Beginner's Mind,* Boston: Shambala. 2006.

Suzman, James, *Affluence Without Abundance: The Disappearing World of the Bushmen,* New York: Bloomsbury, 2017.

Swartz, David, *Culture & Power: The Sociology of Pierre Bourdieu,* Chicago: University of Chicago Press, 1997.

Swimme, Brian Thomas and Mary Evelyn Tucker, *Journey of the Universe,* New Haven: Yale University Press, 2011.

Thurman, Howard, *Jesus and the Disinherited,* Boston: Beacon Press, 1976.

Tillich, Paul, *The Courage to Be,* New Haven, Yale University Press, 1952.

Trungpa, Chogyam, *Cutting Through Spiritual Materialism,* Boston: Shambala, 2008.

Vernezze, Peter and Carl J. Porter, *Bob Dylan and Philosophy,* Chicago: Open Court, 2006.

West, Cornel, *Democracy Matters: Winning the Fight Against Imperialism.* New York: Penguin Books, 2004.

Wilber, Ken, *Trump in a Post-Truth World,* Boulder: Shambala Publications, 2017.

Winograd, Morley and Michael D. Hais, *Millennial Momentum: How a New Generation is Remaking America,* New Brunswick: Rutgers University Press, 2011.

Resources

The following projects are engaged in efforts related to the proposals offered in this draft declaration.

- Better Angels https://better-angels.org/
- Bridge Alliance http://www.bridgealliance.us/
- Center for Contemplative Mind in Society http://www.contemplativemind.org/
- Center for Transformative Change https://www.facebook.com/centerxchange/
- CivilPolitics.org http://www.civilpolitics.org/
- East Point Peace Academy http://eastpointpeace.org/
- Generative Somatics http://www.generativesomatics.org/
- GLIDE Memorial Church https://www.glide.org/home
- Ignite Institute https://www.igniteatpsr.com/
- Interaction Institute for Social Change http://www.interactioninstitute.org/
- Living Room Conversations https://livingroomconversations.org/
- #LoveArmy https://www.lovearmy.org/
- Metta Center for Nonviolence https://mettacenter.org/
- Moral Mondays https://en.wikipedia.org/wiki/Moral_Mondays
- Movement Strategy Center http://movementstrategy.org/
- Mujeres Unidas y Activas (MUA) http://mujeresunidas.net/
- National Domestic Workers Alliance https://www.domesticworkers.org/
- Network of Spiritual Progressives (NSP)

https://spiritualprogressives.org/
- OUR Walmart https://www.united4respect.org
- Pachamama Alliance ttps://www.pachamama.org/
- People's Suppers https://thepeoplessupper.org/
- Poor People's Campaign
  https://poorpeoplescampaign.org/
- Rockwood Leadership Institute
  rockwoodleadership.org
- Shift Network https://theshiftnetwork.com/
- Social Transformation Project http://stproject.org/
- The Village Square https://tlh.villagesquare.us/
- Thrive East Bay http://www.thriveeastbay.org/
- Work That Reconnects Network
  https://workthatreconnects.org/

Acknowledgements

During this draft declaration's composition, the following individuals provided valuable support: Yahya Abdal-Aziz, Sara Colm, Steve Gerritson, Joan Greenfield, David Hartsough, Mary Hudson, Mike Larsen, Carol Lopez, Genevieve Marcus, Bob Morgan, Dan Nissenbaum, and Jakob Possert. During the last few weeks, Steve Gerritson offered helpful suggestions concerning content, proofread everything, and discussed key issues.

Last November, in response to the first draft, which was titled "Transform the World with Holistic Communities: Personal, Social, Cultural, and Political," in addition to those listed above, the following individuals offered constructive criticisms, suggestions, or words of encouragement: Rosa Beléndez, Dorsey Blake, John Breeding, Michael Carano, Jim Costa, Katherine Forrest, Joshua Gorman, Lani Kaahumanu, Paul Kinburn, Paul Kleyman, Alan Levin, Mary Kay Magistad, Roger Marsden, Mike Miller, Kitty Myers, Michael Nagler, Carol Norris, Liz Olson, Daisy Ozim, Jed Riffe, Anjali Sawhney, Jack Sawyer, Randy Schutt, Melinda Stone, and Gary Vondran. And Bob Anschuetz provided extensive copy-editing.

I also express my special gratitude to others still living who've supported and influenced me over the years through personal interactions: Ajahn Amaro, Frank Bardacke, Joyce Beattie, Dan Brook, Ted Chabasinksi, Michael Doughty, Charla Drake, Sandi Gonzales, Kazu Haga, Roy Harrison, Jan Hartsough, Taj James, Sharon Johnson, Janelle Jones, William Kruse, Chris Moore-Backman, Eva Paterson, Chris Price, Dusa Althea Rammessirsingh, Dave Robbins, Brenda Salgado, Rob Waters, and Rev. Cecil Williams.

I give particular "shout outs" to Roma Guy, an ally since we served on the Baker Places Board of Directors in the early

1970s, Rhonda Magee, a fellow Emersonian whose insightful support has been extremely valuable, Rebecca Crabb, my psychotherapist whose wisdom has aided me throughout, David Wallace, who designed the cover with a key assist from Sara Colm, and my sister, Mary Hudson, my longest living soul mate.

Most of all, I thank my mother, the Holy Spirit, and Mother Nature, without whom none of this would have been possible.

About the Author

In 1962, a student housing co-op introduced Wade Lee Hudson to the cooperative movement. In 1963, a James Baldwin lecture inspired him to become immersed in the civil rights movement. In 1964, working full-time for twelve months as an orderly in a psychiatric institution opened his heart even further. In 1965, meditation, massage, backpacking, psychodrama, *Varieties of Religious Experience* by William James, *I and Thou* by Martin Buber, and *The Courage to Be* by Paul Tillich led him into the human potential movement and spirituality. Ever since, he's focused on integrating those three worlds: the personal, the social, and the political.

In 1967 Wade dedicated his life to organizing communities of faith, love, and action and entered the Pacific School of Religion to prepare for "coffee-house ministries," which were church-funded cultural centers.

There he co-convened the New Seminary Movement, which helped the seminary become less isolated and more involved in the community. After two years, Glide Memorial Church hired him as an Intern Minister and he moved to San Francisco. Since then, he's been a self-taught community organizer.

In addition to engagement in numerous projects led by others, he's initiated or played a major role in these supportive, peer-to-peer communities:

- Alternative Futures Community, which conducted weekend marathons, called Urban Plunges, designed to nurture personal and political transformation.
- Network Against Psychiatric Assault, which opposed forced treatment and facilitated mutual support.
- Muni Coalition, which fought to improve public transit.
- Other Avenues Community Food Store, which evolved into a workers' cooperative.
- District Eleven Residents Association, which did door-to-door precinct work for elections.
- South of Market Grocery, a neighborhood food co-op that provided affordable food to low-income seniors.
- Aarti Cooperative, a low-income housing co-op that empowered tenants.
- Tenderloin Self-Help Center, which served the low-income Tenderloin neighborhood.
- 509 Cultural Center, which evolved into the award-winning Luggage Store Gallery.
- *The Tenderloin Times*, a groundbreaking, multi-language neighborhood newspaper.
- Solutions to Poverty Workshop, which developed a ten-point program to end poverty in the United States and evolved into the Campaign to Abolish Poverty.
- Internet Learning Center, which served low-income residents during the early days of the Internet.

- San Francisco Progressive Challenge, which promoted the Fairness Agenda for America developed by the Institute for Policy Studies.
- Reaching Beyond the Choir Project and What We Believe Network, which aimed to articulate core values and principles that could be broadly embraced.
- Charter for Compassion Network, which aimed to advance the Charter throughout society with political action.
- Iraq Peace Team, which opposed the Iraq War as witnesses in Baghdad during the invasion.
- Occupy Be the Change Caucus, which pushed Occupy San Francisco to embrace deep nonviolence and experimented with mutual support methods.
- Western Park Residents Council, which established a partnership with management to improve residents' quality of life.

With those projects, underlying personal and spiritual values were often implicit and not clearly agreed on. In 2004, Wade decided to explore how progressive activists might be more effective. He then initiated four Strategy Workshops, two Compassionate Politics Workshops, and a Gandhi-King Three-fold Path Workshop — and participated in numerous workshops on related issues convened by others. This draft declaration continues along that path.

Wade has published four books:

- *Economic Security for All: How to End Poverty in the United States*, 1996.
  http://shults.org/wadehudson/esfa/.
- *Baghdad Journal,* Inlet Publications, 2003.
- *Global Transformation: Strategy for Action*, iUniverse, 2007.
- *My Search for Deep Community: An Autobiography*, 2014. http://www.deepcommunity.org/

and two booklets:

- *Promoting the General Welfare: A Campaign for American Values*, 2004.
- *The Compassion Movement: A Declaration*, Charter for Compassion Network, 2010.

Notes

[1] Quoted in Banville, John, "The Most Entertaining Philosopher," *The New York Review of Books,"* Oct 27, 2011. 41.

[2] "Filmmaker Interview — Karen Thorsen," *American Masters*, Nov 29, 2006.

[3] "Elizabeth Warren: 'The System Is Rigged,'" *The Atlantic*, Sep 6, 2012.

[4] "Trump told workers that the system is rigged. Now he's showing them just how much," *Washington Post*, Sep 4, 2017.

[5] "The Populist Prophet," *New Yorker,* Oct 12, 2015.

[6] Retrieved from https://charterforcompassion.org/.

[7] Retrieved from http://www.un.org/en/universal-declaration-human-rights/.

[8] Retrieved from http://www.thekingcenter.org/king-philosophy.

[9] Retrieved from http://stproject.org/about-us/who-we-work-with/.

[10] Retrieved from https://en.wikipedia.org/wiki/Twelve-step_program.

[11] "Our Elites Still Don't Get It," *The New York Times,* Nov 16, 2017.

[12] "Money has too much of an influence in politics, Americans say," *MSNBC*, June 2, 2015.

[13] Samuel Bowles and Herbert Gintis, "The Inheritance of Inequality," *Journal of Economic Perspectives*, 16:3, Summer 2002, 3-30.

[14] "What is intersectionality, and what does it have to do with me?", YW Boston, March 29, 2017.

[15] "Why Wages Aren't Growing," Bloomberg, Sep 21, 2017.

[16] "How Technology Is Destroying Jobs," MIT Technology Review, June 12, 2013.

[17] "The Destructive Dynamics of Political Tribalism," *The New York Times,* Feb 20, 2018.

[18] "World is losing the battle against climate change, Macron says," Reuters, Dec 11, 2017.

[19] Putnam, Robert D., *Bowling Alone: The Collapse and Revival of American Community*, 2000.

[20] "Americans Have Fewer Friends Outside the Family, Duke Study Shows," Duke Today, June 23, 2006.

[21] Twenge, Jean M. "The Narcissism Epidemic," Psychology Today, Retrieved from https://www.psychologytoday.com/blog/the-narcissism-epidemic.

[22] "Why a 'war' on terrorism will generate yet more terrorism," The Guardian, Nov 30, 2015.

[23] Google "polls backed by majorities of Republicans, Independents, and Democrats."

[24] Kahane, Adam, *Collaborating with the Enemy: How to Work with People You Don't Agree with or Like or Trust*, Oakland: Berrett-Koehler, 2017.

[25] Suzman, James, *Affluence Without Abundance: The Disappearing World of the Bushmen*m 46-50.

[26] Suzman, James, 28.

[27] Wikipedia, "Hunter-gatherer," Retrieved from https://en.wikipedia.org/wiki/Hunter-gatherer.

[28] Wikipedia, "Dominance hierarchy," Retrieved from https://en.wikipedia.org/wiki/Dominance_hierarchy.

[29] Haidt, Jonathan, *The Righteous Mind.*

[30] Suzman, 8.

[31] Scott, James C., *Against the Grain: A Deep History of the Earliest States.* (This section of the draft declaration draws heavily on this book.).

[32] Wikipedia, "Social dominance theory," Retrieved from https://en.wikipedia.org/wiki/Social_dominance_theory.

[33] "How Humans Became 'Consumers': A History," The Atlantic, Nov 28, 2016

[34] Wikipedia, "Golden Age," Retrieved from https://en.wikipedia.org/wiki/Golden_Age.

[35] See Wikipedia, "Diggers." Retrieved from https://en.wikipedia.org/wiki/Diggers.

[36] Isenberg, Nancy, *White Trash: The 400-year Untold History of Class in America,* 30.

[37] Isenberg, 98.

[38] Tutu, Desmond and 14th Dalai Lama, *The Book of Joy,* p.135.

[39] "The Art and Business of Motivational Speaking," Inc. magazine, Retrieved from https://www.inc.com/magazine/20101201/the-art-and-business-of-motivational-speaking_pagen_2.html.

[40] Lawrimore,, E. W. "Buck" *The 5 Keys To Unlimited Success & Happiness,* 2011.

[41] Wikipedia, "Prosperity theology/Recent History," Retrieved from https://en.wikipedia.org/wiki/Prosperity_theology#Recent_history.

[42] "Why Grading on the Curve Hurts," *Teaching Community*, Retrieved from http://teaching.monster.com/benefits/articles/5658-why-grading-on-the-curve-hurts.

[43] "The Culture of Celebrity," Psychology Today, Retrieved from https://www.psychologytoday.com/articles/199505/the-culture-celebrity.

[44] "Winning isn't everything; it's the only thing," Retrieved from https://en.wikipedia.org/wiki/Winning_isn%27t_everything;_it%27s_the_only_thing.

[45] "Selective Paternalism," AMA Journal of Ethics, July 2012, Volume 14, Number 7: 582-588. For a commentary on the shift away from the prior era that was "steeped in medical paternalism," see "For Doctors, Age May Be More Than a Number," The New York Times, Jan 6, 2018.

[46] "The New Paternalism," Brookings, Oct 1, 1997.

[47] Over the years, I've heard this principle affirmed informally many times. For a discussion of it related to business, see Gamal Newry, "We must learn from past tragedy, by preparing for it!" Retrieved from http://preventativemeasures.org/we-must-learn-from-past-tragedy-by-preparing-for-it.

[48] "The Mobility Myth," New Yorker, March 3, 2014.

[49] "Yes, the Rich Are Different," Pew Research Center, Aug 27, 2012.

[50] "Poll: The Rich Deserve Their Wealth," CNBC, July 13, 2012.

[51] "Who Wants To Be Rich?", Pew Research Center, April 30. 2008.

[52] "System," Merriam-Webster. Retrieved from https://www.merriam-webster.com/dictionary/system.

[53] "System: more than the sum of its parts," e-tech, Retrieved from https://iecetech.org/issue/2013-01/System-more-than-the-sum-of-its-parts.

[54] "Nonlinear Causality," Complexity Labs, Retrieved from http://complexitylabs.io/nonlinear-causality/.

[55] "Anthropology Chapter 1," Quizlet, Retrieved from https://quizlet.com/89641292/anthropology-chapter-1-flash-cards/.

[56] "Ecosystems, Organisms, and Machines," BioScience, Retrieved from https://academic.oup.com/bioscience/article/55/12/1069/407146.

[57] Retrieved from http://www.innovationlabs.com/2007/10/the-purpose-of-a-system-is-what-it-does/.

[58] Garner, Roberta and Black Hawk Hancock, ed. *Social Theory: Continuity and Confrontation: A Reader*, 2014. "Society can be understood as a system; sociology is the study of social systems, which are coherent and relatively stable over time."

[59] "The Globalization of Politics: American Foreign Policy for a New Century," Brookings, Jan 1, 2003.

[60] Wikipedia, "Pierre Bourdieu," Retrieved from https://en.wikipedia.org/wiki/Pierre_Bourdieu.

[61] "What is Rankism and Why Do We "Do" It?", Huffington Post, May 25, 2011.

[62] Haidt, 198-201.

[63] "Tuning In: Improving Your Listening Skills," Wall Street Journal, July 22, 2014.

[64] "Empathy: College students don't have as much as they used to," Michigan News, May 27, 2010.

[65] Wikipedia, "Expressions of dominance," Retrieved from https://en.wikipedia.org/wiki/Expressions_of_dominance.

[66] Stulp, Gert, Abraham P. Buunk, Simon Verhulst, and Thomas V. Pollet, "Human Height Is Positively Related to Interpersonal Dominance in Dyadic Interactions," PLOS,Retrieved from https://www.ncbi.nlm.nih.gov/pmc/articles/PMC4342156/.

[67] Retrieved from https://www.shmoop.com/streetcar-named-desire/society-class-quotes-3.html.

[68] "Do Millennial Men Want Stay-at-Home Wives?", The New York Times, March 31, 2017.

[69] Frank, Robert H., *Success and Luck: Good Fortune and the Myth of Meritocracy.* Also see "Why Luck Matters More Than You Might Think," The Atlantic, May 2016 and "Why the myth of a perfect meritocracy is so pernicious," Vox, Dec 15, 2017.

[70] "Are marriages stronger when one spouse is dominant?", The Telegraph, Feb 7, 2015.

[71] Kripal, Jeffrey J., *Esalen: America and the Religion of No Religion,* 286-7.

[72] Institute for the Study of Race and Ethnicity, "Implicit Bias Review 2015." Retrieved from http://kirwaninstitute.osu.edu/research/understanding-implicit-bias/.

[73] "Study: lighter-skinned black and Hispanic people look smarter to white people," Vox, Feb 28, 2015.

[74] "Dangerous idiots: how the liberal media elite failed working-class Americans," The Guardian, Oct 13, 2016.

[75] "America is held hostage by flyover states," The Hill, Dec 12, 2016.

[76] "12 Women Who Say Sexual Harassment Cost Them Their Careers," Time, Nov 15. 2017.

[77] "The Challenge of Paternalism in Social Work," Social Work Today, January/February 2005.

[78] "The Real Lesson of the Stanford Prison Experiment," New Yorker, June 12, 2015.

[79] "Why America Must Lead," The Catalyst, Winter 2016.

[80] See https://www.holacracy.org/.

[81] Rutherford Insitute, "Transforming America's Schools into Authoritarian Instruments of Compliance," Oct 7, 2013.

[82] "Economic Inequality: It's Far Worse Than You Think," Scientific American, March 31, 2015.

[83] "Close Friends Less Common Today, Study Finds," Live Science, Nov 4, 2011.

[84] "How Social Isolation Is Killing Us," The New York Times, December 22, 2016.

[85] "We're eating more of our meals alone: Is that a bad thing?", Today.com, Aug. 25, 2015.

[86] "Happiness Is Other People," The New York Times, Oct 27, 2017.

[87] Steptoe, Andrew , Aparna Shankar, Panayotes Demakakos and Jane Wardle, "Social isolation, loneliness, and all-cause mortality in older men and women," Retrieved from https://doi.org/10.1073/pnas.1219686110.

[88] "Guns and Opioids Are American Scourges Fueled by Availability," The New York Times, Feb 24, 2018.

[89] "Why Access to Screens Is Lowering Kids' Social Skills," Time, Aug 21, 2014.

[90] Personal communication.

[91] Retrieved from https://www.nobelprize.org/nobel_prizes/literature/laureates/1990/paz-lecture.html.

[92] Other sources of concern included: The United States was losing the Vietnam War, which called into question its future global power; More consumer and environmental regulations might further restrain their freedom; Labor unions were conducting more strikes and pushing for higher wages; Many formerly dependent countries were demanding and achieving independence; From October 1973 to March 1974, an Arab oil embargo targeted at pro-Israel nations caused the price of oil to rise from $3 per barrel to nearly $12.

[93] Saez Emmanuel and Gabriel Zucman, "Wealth Inequality in the United States since 1913: Evidence from Capitalized Income Tax Data," NBER Working Paper No. 20625, October 2014.

[94] Retrieved from http://constitutionus.com/.

[95] "What We Owe to Others: Simone Weil's Radical Reminder, *The New York Times,* Feb 20, 2018.

[96] Retrieved from https://incommunion.org/wp-content/uploads/2005/04/Pogo.jpg?w=240.

[97] Retrieved from https://apomm.net/2017/02/14/claudia-horwitz/

[98] "What Could Raising Taxes on the 1% Do? Surprising Amounts," The New York Times, Oct 16, 2015.

[99] Suzman, 185.

[100] "10 ways white people are more racist than they realize," Alternet, March 4, 2015.

[101] Wikipedia, "Citizens United v. FEC." Retrieved from https://en.wikipedia.org/wiki/Citizens_United_v._FEC.

[102] Retrieved from https://participedia.net/en/methods/deliberative-polling.

[103] "Mission, Vision and Values," Centre for Justice and Reconciliation. Retrieved from http://restorativejustice.org/#sthash.rELDBcH0.dpbs.

[104] Wikipedia, "Conflict resolution," Retrieved from https://en.wikipedia.org/wiki/Conflict_resolution.

[105] See https://www.holacracy.org/.

[106] https://en.wikipedia.org/wiki/Social_entrepreneurship

[107] Retrieved from http:// http://worldhappiness.report/.

[108] "5 'Radical' Bernie Sanders Ideas Many Americans Strongly Support," Alternet, July 5, 2015.

[109] "Outsmarting Our Primitive Responses to Fear," The New York Times, Oct 26, 2017.

[110] Wikipedia, "Sticks and Stones," Retrieved from https://en.wikipedia.org/wiki/Sticks_and_Stones.

[111] Thurman, Howard, *Jesus and the Disinherited,* 28.

[112] Tutu, Desmond and 14th Dalai Lama, *The Book of Joy.*

[113] Retrieved from https://www.biblegateway.com/passage/?search=Matthew+18:2-4.

[114] Kahane, *Collaborating with the Enemy*, 96.

[115] Wikipedia, "History of United States antitrust law," Retrieved from https://en.wikipedia.org/wiki/History_of_United_States_antitrust_law.

[116] "Capitalism's secret love affair with bureaucracy," Financial Times, March 6, 2015.

[117] Retrieved from https://www.merriam-webster.com/dictionary/lead.

[118] John C. Maxwell, Retrieved from https://www.brainyquote.com/quotes/john_c_maxwell_383606?src=t_leader.

[119] Dwight Eisenhower, Retrieved from https://www.nytimes.com/2017/12/29/opinion/donald-trump-reality-tv.html.

[120] Ronald Heifetz, Retrieved from https://www.npr.org/2013/11/11/230841224/lessons-in-leadership-its-not-about-you-its-about-them.

[121] Ken Blanchard, Retrieved from https://ideas.bkconnection.com/bk-broadcast/my-top-7-servant-leadership-summit-learnings-takeaways.

[122] Daniel Krauthammer, "What Makes America Great?", Retrieved from, Retrieved from http://www.weeklystandard.com/what-makes-america-great/article/2007818.

[123] Robert Gass, *Transforming Organizations,* 103.

[124] Gary Wills, Retrieved from http://www.goalgettingpodcast.com/qod-188-leader-one-mobilizes-others-toward-shared-goal-gary-wills/.

[125] Retrieved from https://www.merriam-webster.com/dictionary/leadership.

[126] "Most leaders die with their mouths open," TechRepublic, April 5, 2011.

[127] "Most leaders die with their mouths open," TechRepublic, April 5, 2011.

[128] "The Art of Chaordic Leadership," Leader to Leader, 2000, by Dee Hock.

[129] "The Art of Chaordic Leadership," Leader to Leader, 2000, by Dee Hock

[130] Carver, John and Miriam Carver, "The Policy Governance® Model, Retrieved from http://www.carvergovernance.com/model.htm.

[131] Retrieved from https://www.holacracy.org/.

[132] "Beyond the Holacracy Hype," Harvard Business Review, July-Aug 2016.

[133] Wikipedia, "The Tyranny of Structurelessness," Retrieved from https://en.wikipedia.org/wiki/The_Tyranny_of_Structurelessness.

[134] Retrieved from https://thenextsystem.org/.

[135] Wikipedia, "Benefit corporation," Retrieved from https://en.wikipedia.org/wiki/Benefit_corporation.

[136] Rosenberg, Tina, Join the Club: How Peer Pressure Can Transform the World, xi-xxiv.

[137] Suzman, 179-80.

[138] George, Bill and Doug Baker, *True North Groups: A Powerful Path to Personal and Leadership Development.* Retrieved from http://www.billgeorge.org/true-north-groups/.

[139] "Principles of Harm Reduction," Harm Reduction Coalition. Retrieved from http://harmreduction.org/about-us/principles-of-harm-reduction/.

[140] Retrieved from http://www.un.org/en/universal-declaration-human-rights/.

[141] Retrieved from https://www.space.com/17307-neil-armstrong-one-small-step-quote.html.

[142] Haidt, J., *The Righteous Mind: Why Good People Are Divided by Politics and Religion,* 2012, 251.

Made in the USA
Middletown, DE
26 October 2022

13586283R00064